PARENTS EXIST, OK!?
Issues and visions for parent-school relationships

Joe Hallgarten

30-32 Southampton St
London WC2E 7RA
Tel: 020 7470 6100
Fax: 020 7470 6111
postmaster@ippr.org.uk
www.ippr.org
Registered charity 800065

The Institute for Public Policy Research is an independent charity whose purpose is to contribute to public understanding of social, economic and political questions through research, discussion and publication. It was established in 1988 by leading figures in the academic, business and trade-union communities to provide an alternative to the free market think tanks.

IPPR's research agenda reflects the challenges facing Britain and Europe. Current programmes cover the areas of economic and industrial policy, Europe, governmental reform, human rights, defence, social policy, the environment and media issues.

Besides its programme of research and publication, IPPR also provides a forum for political and trade union leaders, academic experts and those from business, finance, government and the media, to meet and discuss issues of common concern.

Trustees

Lord Eatwell (Chairman)
Gail Rebuck (Secretary)
Lord Gavron (Treasurer)
Lord Alli
Professor Tony Atkinson
Professor Kumar Bhattacharyya
Rodney Bickerstaffe
Lord Brooke
John Edmonds

Professor Anthony Giddens
Jeremy Hardie
Lord Hollick
Jane Humphries
Professor David Marquand
Frances O'Grady
Chris Powell
Jan Royall
Baroness Young of Old Scone

Production & design by **EMPHASIS**
ISBN 1 86030 125 8
© IPPR 2000

Printed and bound in Great Britain by Biddles Ltd, *www.biddles.co.uk*

Contents

About the author
Preface

Introduction 1

I: EVIDENCE AND CONTEXTS

1. Do parents matter? 9
2. Changing family and social contexts 19

II: FAMILY AND SCHOOL AS MUTUAL SUPPORT MECHANISMS

3. Home-school communication 34
4. School-based support 49
5. Home-based support 62

III: EXIT AND VOICE

6. Parental choice 78
7. Parental voice 92
8. A framework for whole-school change 107

APPENDICES

Appendix 1: Teachers and parents: a survey of teachers' views 121

Appendix 2: Wednesbury Education Action Zone: parents as partners – executive summary by Laura Edwards 125

Appendix 3: Supplementary schooling in the CfBT/Lambeth Education Action Zone – a summary by Dr John Bastiani 131

Bibliography 139

About the author

Joe Hallgarten is a teacher and Research Fellow in education policy at the Institute for Public Policy Research. He has taught in primary schools in Wythenshawe, Lambeth and Islington. His current research interests include the future of the teaching profession, digital media and education, and Education Action Zones. He is the co-editor, with Nick Pearce, of *Tomorrow's Citizens: Critical Debates in Education*.
j.hallgarten@ippr.org.uk

Preface

This publication is the result of a project undertaken by IPPR between May 1999 and May 2000. Many conclusions are provisional and have been put forward to stimulate further discussion and research. The publication aims to be accessible to as wide an audience as possible, including teachers and parents. It is hoped that this publication will begin a process of wider, deeper thinking about parent-school relationships.

The project took the form of an investigation, although three pieces of primary research were carried out. Summaries of all of these are included in the appendices and the full research reports are available on IPPR's website at www.ippr.org.

The author would like to thank all those who have contributed to the ideas contained in this volume, through discussions, seminars, and project visits. Families and schools are subjects that everyone seems to hold strong opinions about. Combine them, and the number and diversity of opinions seemed to more than double! I would particularly like to thank the following, who gave valuable advice and support:

John Bastiani, who worked as external consultant to the project, Sheila Dainton (Association of Teachers and Lecturers), Sue Aclam-Hood, Nick Baxter, Colin Curtis, Grainne McQuillan and Nick Pearce (DfEE), Jeremy Hardie, Lisa Harker, Matthew Taylor, Peter Robinson and Helena Scott (IPPR), Geena Gardiner (Parklands Junior School), Sally Power (Institute for Education), Belinda Appiah (The Runneymede Trust), Patricia Clark (Avondale Park Primary School), Titus Alexander, Sheila Wolfendale (University of East London), Margaret Tulloch (Campaign for State Education), Jacquie Disney (Parents Information Network), Sue Barnes (Leicester EAZ), Tim Coulson (CfBT/Lambeth EAZ), Neil Sortwell (Wednesbury EAZ), Barbara Hearn (National Children's Bureau), Lisa Capper (CEDC), Molly Evans (Family Friends), Toby Greany (Campaign for Learning), Mary Crowley (Parenting Education and Support Forum), Heather Du Quesnay (National College for School Leadership), Ros Edwards (South Bank University), Ken Worpole (Comedia), Emma Westcott (General Teaching Council), Gavin Davies, Jerramy Fine, Catherine Ravenscroft and Loan Truong. Naturally, none of the above carries any responsibility for the final version, which rests with the author alone.

IPPR gratefully acknowledges financial support for this project from CfBT Education Services and the Department for Education and Employment. In addition IPPR acknowledges the financial support of the following organisations: The Association of Teachers and Lecturers (for the ATL/IPPR teachers survey); the CfBT/Lambeth Education Action Zone (for the research on supplementary schools); the Wednesbury Education Action Zone and Paul Hamlyn Foundation (for the research in the Wednesbury Education Action Zone).

for Sylvie

Introduction

I have given you more power than you have ever had or dreamed of.
Kenneth Baker, then Secretary of State for Education, addressing a group of parents, 1988 (in Holden *et al*, 1994)

PARENTS EXIST, OK!?
Graffiti painted on the outside wall of a Hackney primary school, 1998

This book explores current and future challenges and opportunities for the relationships between parents and their children's schools. In a time of rapid change, both in the educational world and beyond, home-school relationships seem a constant foundation upon which the success of schools is built or crumbles.

How strong are the foundations? In many schools visited during the project, incredibly strong, and clearly sustainable. However, it is equally clear that many schools are in real need of guidance and support. In 1996, Bastiani wrote that 'singly, or together, government legislation or administrative requirements do not offer either an adequate or credible vision of how things might be, or a satisfactory basis for the planning of a school's work with parents' (Bastiani & Wolfendale, 1996: 59). Four years on, in spite of the priority this government has given to education in its thinking, policies and investment, this seems as true now as it did then. By unpicking all the moments when parents and schools can and could collide, this report aims to generate proposals that policy makers, practitioners and parents will need to consider, if such a vision is to be created.

The book presents new proposals for the extension and enrichment of parental involvement in their children's learning, but this is only one strand of its approach. This is because there is already an enormous amount of current activity, at national, local and school levels, which aims to promote such involvement and change parental attitudes to suit the needs of pupils and schools. As Merttens writes, parental involvement is 'the flag we salute whenever it is hoisted' (Merrtens, 1993:2). In a sense, there is no 'policy gap' in this field. There is however an 'evidence gap', since the real impact of much current activity remains unproven.

In contrast, when examining the huge literature on policies and practice in the home-school field, what appears to be lacking is clear analysis of how the promotion of such involvement, combined with other forces, can and should impact on schools as institutions.

The disability rights movement has created a framework for discussing attitudes to disability. In the medical model, the disabled person has to adjust to an institution. In the social model, it is the institution that has to adapt to the needs of the individual. Applying this typology to home-school relations, this report has attempted to use the social model. The onus for change to improve parent-school relationships must fall onto the school, not the parent. The aim should be to create family-like schools, in all their shades of diversity and complexity, not school-like families.

This book is based on two premises; one is that the vast majority of parents want their children to achieve as much as possible at school, and have the will, if not the confidence, to support this ambition through their own actions. The other is that the purpose of any new policies to encourage parental involvement in learning and schools should aim to reduce inequalities in educational outcomes between schools and between individuals. Although the variables are difficult to isolate, the past four decades of rising parental involvement appear to have had the opposite effect.

During the course of this project, many models of parental participation have been suggested, including parents as consumers, partners, collaborators, supporters, problems, solutions, and policemen. This report has borrowed liberally from all of these models. If it has one aspirant model, it is of parents as citizens, with all the rights and responsibilities that this entails. For this to occur, most schools will need to undergo a substantial shift. Power relations between professionals and parents need to be transformed from the current 'command and control' norm to one of 'relational' power, based on collaboration and conversation. The ultimate vision, therefore, is of schools as citizenship banks, where forms of social capital, participation and support can be invested, deposited and withdrawn by all families.

A new political context

> *The involvement of the family in the learning process and the links between home and school are vital to the success we are seeking in raising standards and providing real equality of opportunity.* (Blunkett, D 1998)

New Labour's commitment to raising parents' aspirations for and engagement in their children's learning is not in doubt. Nor, as a few suggest, is this commitment being employed as a cheap option, using parents' precious time to compensate for an underfunded education service. Even if schools reach the nirvana of total effectiveness, this will only account for fifteen per cent of a child's waking hours from birth to sixteen. Parental involvement is seen as a distinct, possibly irreplaceable, influence on children's learning and schools.

There are three strands of government thinking in this area:

- *Encouraging families to learn together* through targeted initiatives such as family learning, and universal national campaigns such as the National Year of Reading and Maths Year 2000.

- *Providing information for parents*, improving the quality of information from and about schools, and about learning itself; this includes a parents' 'rough guide' to the national curriculum.

- *Giving parents a voice*; there are now more parent governors in every school, and at least two parent governors on every LEA's education committee.

In many ways, these policies build on those of the previous government, which had an indisputable interest in the greater participation of parents. However, there has been a substantial change of emphasis. The role of parents as consumers has been given far less attention, although policies and attitudes remain virtually untouched. Market failure is no longer tolerated; schools that have lost the confidence of parents, and find themselves in the vicious circle of falling rolls and low achievement, are given extra resources and support. And resources to encourage parental involvement are skewed towards areas where pupils and parents are most at risk of disaffection from learning in general and schools in particular.

These strategies cannot be viewed in isolation. Good home-school relationships are probably more dependent on policies that may not be directly related to parental involvement. In education, this government has reacted to decades of underinvestment and, for a significant minority of pupils, underachievement, with sustained pressure on and support for schools to raise levels of attainment. Three years on, schools appear to be succeeding on a number of indicators. However, many educators feel forced by the understandable urgency of the government's standards agenda to focus on short-term improvement strategies. For all the rhetoric about encouraging home-school links, the reality, revealed by so many of the people we spoke to during the project, is that many schools have relegated parents down their list of priorities. As one headteacher said, 'home-school links is the long game; you may not see the benefits for years.'

At the same time, public policy towards the family itself is changing. A stable and supportive family environment is increasingly recognised as critical to the development of healthy, well-educated and properly socialised young people. There is, in contrast with the previous administration, an acceptance of the diversity and possibilities of all family structures. There is also a concerted, sustained effort to lift all families out of poverty.

In comparison with their education policies, the family policies of this government appear far more enabling and less prescriptive. The government may fear 'nanny-state' accusations with regards to the family, but not in relation to schools. It is not accidental that the two major policy papers on families and schools were called 'supporting families' and 'excellence in schools'.

Professor Michael Barber has recently written that 'the sustained drive from national government risks the creation of an entirely top-down reform with its associated pressures to conform, whereas all evidence suggests that successful reform requires a combination of top-down and bottom-up change' (Barber, 2000). This report aims to create policies suitable for the second phase of new Labour's education strategy, where the success of most if not all of the top-down reforms should have created the conditions for achievable bottom-up change. 'Intervention in inverse proportion to success', as espoused in *Excellence in Schools*, is the key opportunity for innovative, exciting models of home-school relationships. Home-school relationships should move up the hierarchy of educational priorities at all levels.

A new learning context

Although sometimes masked by this government's necessary concentration on current realities, from improving basic literacy levels to repairing roofs, there is little doubt that the learning landscape will change dramatically during the next few decades. Driven partly by developments in Information and Communications Technology, the education system is crawling from a factory model of schooling to a more polymorphic, flexible model, and finally beginning to take into account different styles of learning and intelligences. This report discusses many current mechanisms and processes that could soon be obsolete. For instance, the ways that achievement is measured and knowledge communicated, the places where learning occurs, and the age-related organisational structure of schooling, are all likely to be transformed. Grounded in current realities, this investigation makes one assumption for the future: that amidst all this change, in decades to come the vast majority of a child's learning will still be carried out within two institutions, the school and the family. For some, this will seem a conservative view, but it is based on the fact that these two institutions have already survived turbulent times and challenges.

Omissions

This book deliberately omits discussion about three key areas. Pre-school learning; parenting education; and inclusion issues, with particular regard to children with special educational needs. The latter is particularly crucial. The best SEN policy and practice, with regards to parents, has often had a significant and positive effect on mainstream work, from individual education plans, to parents' support groups, to LEA parent partnership services, all of which will be in place by 2002. Today's SEN practices are often tomorrow's mainstream ones (see Wolfendale, 1997 & 1999). As far as pre-school learning is concerned, research comprehensively shows that this is the most important time for parental involvement in learning to be encouraged. Current policies acknowledge this, particularly through the SureStart programme, which if successful may have a more positive impact on home-school relationships than any other initiative. Early contact between a school and parents of pre-school age children can build good relationships which continue once the child starts school.

Another area that this book barely covers is that of the pupil perspective on home school relations. The second chapter points out the importance of considering this view, yet research evidence on pupils' opinions is scarce.

The book also avoids using the words 'partnership' and 'community'. Both appear to have become what Vincent describes as:

> Condensation symbols...condensing specific emotions into a particular word or phrase, so that its usage provokes those emotions. However, the exact meanings of the terms are not clearly defined. Indeed, they are often kept vague to attract maximum support. (Vincent, 1996:465)

In the home-school field, 'partnership' seems to have lost all meaning. Perhaps it is a goal that all relationships should define and aspire to, yet never see themselves reaching. As for community, phrases such as 'schools should be community hubs' are easy options, bypassing the real life issues of individual relationships. School's relationships with the collective community are covered elsewhere (see, for example, Ball, 1998); this investigation concentrates on individual relationships between school, parent and child.

The structure of this report

The first part of this book sets out the framework in which home-school relationships are discussed. Chapter 1 investigates the evidence of the 'parent effect' in its many forms. Chapter 2 explores the contexts within which family-school relationships are being formed.

The second part concentrates on current realities and future challenges and opportunities for learning in school and home settings. Home-school communication is the lynchpin upon which all practice in this area relies, and is discussed broadly in chapter 3. Chapters 4 and 5 look in turn at school-based and home-based support that families and schools offer each other.

The third part examines parental choice and voice, two issues that may seem remote and less relevant to children's learning. However, both are crucial to the formation of family-school relationships. The concluding chapter introduces a wider discussion about cultural change in schools. Staffing issues are given particular attention. The appendices contain summaries of three pieces of research that have been carried out during this project.

I: Evidence and contexts

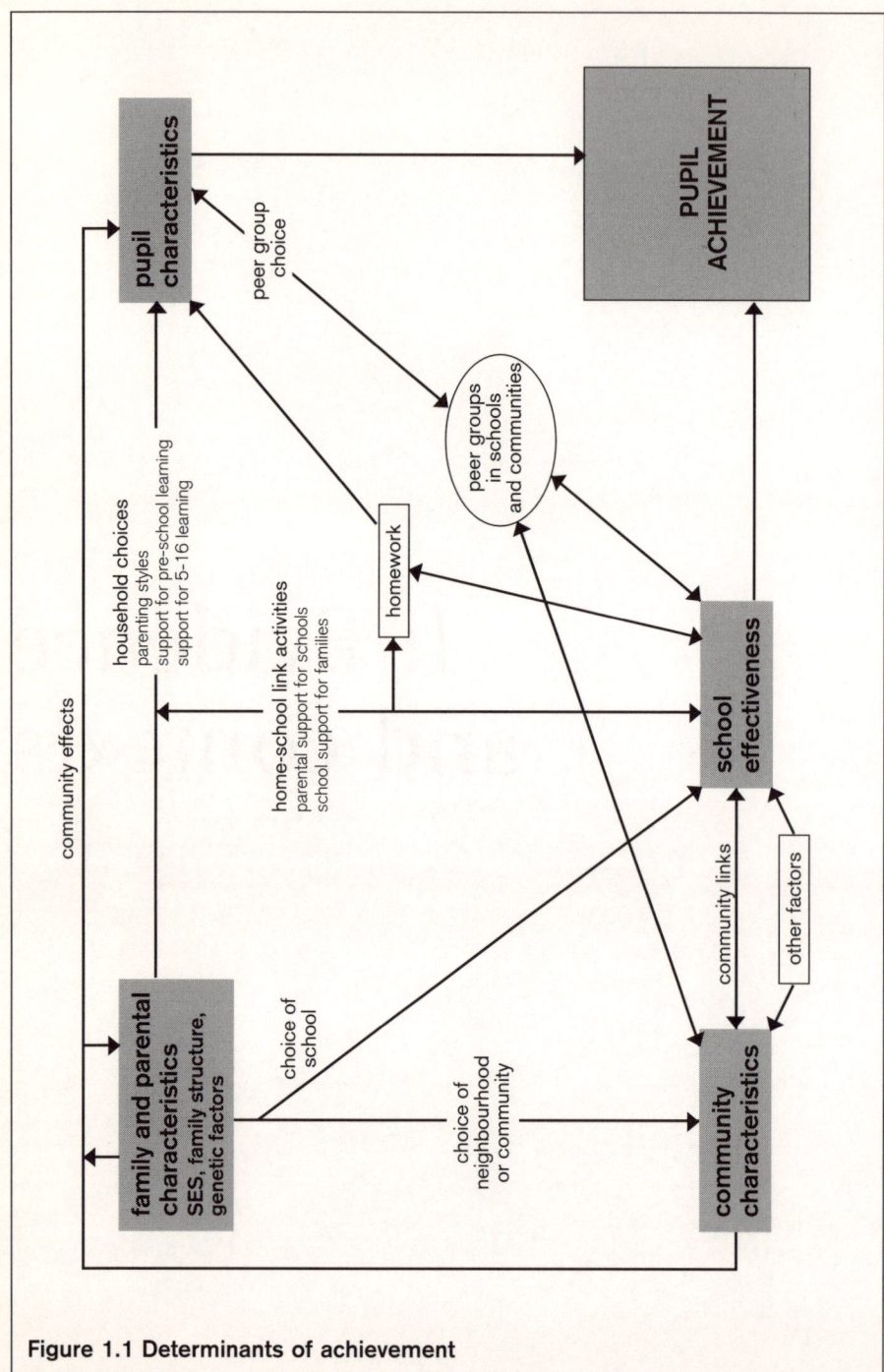

Figure 1.1 Determinants of achievement

1. Do parents matter?

Which factors contribute towards creating an effective learner or an effective school? Wolfendale writes that 'Educational achievement or underachievement rests upon a complex multifactorial matrix' (Bastiani & Wolfendale, 2000:1). Figure 1.1 attempts to map this matrix. However, the variables are more difficult to unmesh than this chart indicates.

What unites these variables is that parents have some influence, if not necessarily ownership or a feeling of control, over all of them. This chapter briefly outlines current thinking on these factors, before focussing on the parental involvement question.

Socio-economic status (SES)

At whatever stage educational achievement is measured, achievement in the UK appears directly proportionate to the socio-economic status (SES) of a child's parents. This starts from birth; a social class gradient in cognitive development can be identified at 22 months, and steadily increases (Feinstein, 1998). Yet this does not prove a causal link between the two. Research has attempted to isolate the multiple factors that contribute to SES.

The most reliable indicators of a child's educational performance are the qualifications of his parents, and levels of poverty. Analysis of the National Child Development Study (NCDS) has shown the most significant factors for post-sixteen participation to be whether a child's parents left school at sixteen, and whether the family has been in financial difficulties (Gregg & Machin, 1998). Statistics also consistently show a clear link between the poor basic skills of young people and the lack of qualifications of their parents (Elkinsmyth & Bynner, 1994; Moser, 1999).

Eligibility for free school meals is a strong predictor of low educational attainment. But aside from families in poverty, it is difficult to establish a link between raw family income levels and pupil performance. There is strong statistical evidence that, once basic needs are met, parental income has little correlation with child outcomes (Mayer, 1997; Blau, 1999). Mayer argues that during three decades of increasing financial inequality in the US, inequalities in attainment have not risen and may even have narrowed (except amongst the American 'underclass'). The NCDS has shown that the impact of parental unemployment on attainment is limited, once poverty is controlled for.

Research into the effects of parental employment on pupils' achievement has mainly focused on the employment of mothers. The evidence is far from unanimous; in particular, there is little consensus over the effect of maternal employment during a child's early years. However, recent longitudinal studies suggest that maternal employment during a child's school years has a positive effect. Research using the

British Household Panel Study has shown that maternal employment during childhood is associated with favourable outcomes during young adulthood: higher educational attainments, and smaller chances of unemployment (Ermisch & Franseconi, 1998). This is supported by NCDS data (Robertson & Symons, 1996). A comprehensive review of American birth cohort studies asserts that maternal employment tends to have a positive impact on achievement, but that a mother's role satisfaction is a far more important determinant of a child's achievement than her employment status (Moore *et al*, 1999). The same study points more directly to a positive link between a father's employment status and his children's educational performance. There is some agreement that any reduction in time resources for working parents can be compensated for by increases in material resources and other factors such as improved social contact and forms of cultural, human and social capital.

Harmonising this evidence into policy considerations is awkward. In particular, more analysis is needed to take into account the unintended impact of other social policies on educational performance. For instance, will the current attempt to lift families out of poverty through the Working Families Tax Credit and other 'welfare to work' policies have any effect on the educational motivations and achievements of these families? What is a more efficient way to spend money if the purpose is to raise poor children's achievements: lifting their parents out of poverty? providing opportunities for their parents to gain qualifications? or increasing their local school's resources? Amongst these big questions, the parental involvement question can often appear as a sideshow, a distraction from wider family and welfare policy questions.

Family structure

All of the large-scale studies above are unanimous in agreeing that, once other socio-economic variables are taken into account, lone parenthood is an insignificant factor in determining pupil outcomes. For instance, analyses of Youth Cohort Studies (YCS) find no evidence that lone parenthood reduces school staying-on rates (Rice, 1996). Although a study based on the BHPS reveals that 'experience of life in a non-intact family is usually associated with disadvantaged outcomes of young adults', it also concedes that this is almost entirely due to the socio-economic circumstances of many single parent or disrupted families (Ermisch & Franseconi, 1997).

At the same time, studies across international data sets have shown a strong correlation between family breakdown and low achievement, even if remarriage occurs after a divorce. There is also strong evidence that boys who have no contact with their fathers are more likely to underachieve at school (McLanahan, 1997; Wylie & Thomson, 1999). Although much of this correlation may again be due to other variables (for instance, financial problems and relocation after breakdown), this may be an area for substantial policy levers. If the current education system is disadvantaging children from non-traditional families, or families who are more mobile, then the system itself must adapt.

Nechyba *et al*'s review of statistical impacts of family variables on child outcomes argues that the following factors are weak or unproved: birth order, lone parenthood and parental age. They argue that family size may be relevant, due to the effect of 'resource dilution' on families. This final point concurs with a YCS analysis showing that sixteen year olds from large families are less likely to continue with their education (Rice, 1996).

There is a dearth of research evidence concerning the impact of more fluid 'families of choice' on educational performance. Research has tended to focus on the difference between 'intact' and 'disrupted' families, a distinction that is becoming increasingly blurred. Family structures are becoming more flexible, with the increasing use of part time or 'supply' parents. Although there is strong anecdotal evidence that, for instance, children living in extended families perform well at school, this has not yet been extracted from concurrent factors.

Genetic effects

Advances in brain science and genetics have made it more difficult and unnecessary to deny hereditary influences on academic performance. Studies with twins and siblings estimate that heredity accounts for about fifty per cent of all differences in scholastic achievement (Nechyba *et al*, 1999). This figure is highly disputable, but heredity may prove to be the largest single familial influence on academic achievement.

Excluding data concerning heredity from policy discussions may appear benign; policy should attempt to influence that which is malleable. However, such neglect may lead to a policy bias that militates against redressing educational inequalities. Evidence of genetic influences does not in itself imply that such differences are irremediable. But inequalities of outcome may become increasingly immutable unless policymakers are brave enough to consider genetics in policy formulation.

As our understanding of genetics becomes more sophisticated, opportunities grow for specific, targeted intervention. For instance, meta-analyses of genetic studies indicate that heredity increases in educational importance during middle to late childhood (Plomin & Petrill, 1997). This is just the time when other more explicit family influences may appear to be waning. It may also be the case that certain environments (for instance, the multiple conditions that create social exclusion) may set off triggers that are genetically programmed. Alter the environment, and genetic traits are rendered far less relevant. Nonetheless, as research continues, one can imagine a future Secretary of State for Education pleading with schools that 'poverty of genes is no excuse for failure'.

Family and parental characteristics

Household choices

So, do the factors considered so far matter intrinsically? Or do they matter because they increase the likelihood of parental involvement in their children's learning and parenting styles, which contribute to a child's success at school? As Mayer's study of educational performance in the US argues, socio-economic factors may be correlated with poor outcomes 'because they are proxies for unmeasured parental characteristics' (Mayer, 1997: 155). These characteristics are far from unmeasured, yet research on 'the parent effect' will always remain largely qualitative; the 'black box' amongst the interconnected grey boxes described above.

Like the whole of this report, the research quoted below focuses on the impact of parental involvement during a pupil's school years. It deliberately ignores two key areas of parental involvement, both of which are worthy of brief consideration:

Pre-school learning

There is an overwhelming research consensus that the quality of a child's pre-school experiences is more crucial to his academic, social, and emotional development than any other 'household choice' factor. New brain research has placed new stress on the relevance of a baby's earliest experiences on educational outcomes. In the years before school, a child's brain is carrying out two key learning activities: making connections and 'pruning' unnecessary connections (Gopnick *et al*, 2000). One study argues that fifty per cent of all learning ability occurs by the age of four, and another thirty per cent in the next four years (Bloom, 1964; Tizard & Hughes, 1984). NCDS analyses show that one of the most significant predictors of post-sixteen staying on rates are reading and maths scores undertaken at age seven (Gregg & Machin, 1998). Unless the 'school effect' during the first two years of schooling is enormous, this again shows the importance of pre-school learning (whether done by parents, other carers or professionals) during the early years.

Moreover, there is proof of the long term effectiveness of intervention programmes during the early years. Research into North American projects such as Head Start and the Michigan High/Scope Nursery education project, has shown that such interventions can not only improve long term achievement of the children involved, but also lead to higher average earnings for the low income families who participate (Fantini, 1980). A longitudinal study of the Perry pre-school project in Michigan has calculated that 'for every dollar spent on the program, seven dollars have been saved in future costs to society' (Schweinhart & Barnes, 1993).

Parenting styles

This encompasses all parenting inputs that do not come under the umbrella of their input into formal learning – a massive area, including shaping behavioural attitudes, creating a 'shared home environment', and creating informal learning opportunities. A case can be strongly argued that parenting styles are key foundations for learning, and thus are far more important than other influences on learning. However, the scope of this report deliberately excludes discussions about 'parenting', the challenge being that schools should aim to maximise children's learning potential and, where possible, form positive relationships with all parents, regardless of diffuse 'parenting styles' (see Pugh *et al*, 1994; Einzig & Wolfendale, 1999; Lloyd, 1999).

The influence of parental support for learning on individual achievement

Three decades of small-scale studies from research for the Plowden Report onwards have consistently flagged parental engagement with their school-aged child's learning as a crucial contributor to individual achievement, particularly in literacy and numeracy (Hannon, 1995). Epstein, reviewing thirty years of North American research, asserted that 'there is consistent evidence that…students gain in personal and academic development if their families emphasise schooling, let their children know they do, and do so continuously over the years.' (Epstein, 1992:473). The evidence seems clear that a lack of interest is a major contributor to underachievement. Home Office Research has shown that truancy is strongly related to low parental interest and poor relationships between parent, child and school (Graham & Bowling, 1995).

Recent longitudinal studies contribute 'harder' evidence to the debate. The National Child Development Study has attempted to measure the 'parental interest' variable. Before discussing the results, it is worth pointing out two weaknesses inherent in them:

- levels of parental interest are assessed through interviews with teachers, which leaves the research open to accusations of positivism.
- research is based on the 1958 and 1970 cohorts; the definition of 'parental involvement' and the dynamics of schools and families have changed considerably since then.

The results are nonetheless useful. Research into children's attainment at secondary school, based on 1958 NCDS data, finds that:

> of the family inputs only the parental interest has a consistently strong impact…the level of interest of the most interested of two parents is crucial. The absence of a parent taking minimum interest has no effect at all…to a great

extent, parental interest explains the variance in attainment otherwise explained by class, [parental] education and family size. (Feinstein & Symons, 1999).

Other NCDS findings show that parental interest can be a protective barrier against other (poverty-related) factors that militate against educational achievement. Hobcraft's study also reveals the importance of paternal interest, especially for boys' achievement, at both ends of the achievement spectrum (Hobcraft, 1998). This is supported by evidence from the North American birth cohort studies cited above.

However, there are growing claims that the impact of active *involvement* with learning, as opposed to interest, is still unproved and may possibly be overstated, particularly in the evaluations of projects that promote such involvement. As Dyson and Robson's recent review claims, evaluations of small-scale projects tend to be far too success-focussed, and often have a veneer of independence that hides the relationship between programme and evaluator (Robson & Dyson, 1999). Evidence from American longitudinal studies has been more mixed than the UK equivalents (Moore *et al*, 1999; Muller, 1993; Sui-Chu & Williams, 1996).

Currently, the identification of parental involvement in a child's education as a key determinant of individual achievement is virtually taken for granted. However, scratch the surface of the research, and the proof seems less cogent. In particular, definitions of what counts as 'involvement', 'engagement' or 'interest' are often vague. If the evidence is fuzzy, there may be serious efficiency and equity questions concerning policies that exhort parents to prioritise formal, school-initiated activities (such as homework) over self-initiated, often less formal, learning opportunities.

Community influences on individual achievement

The assumed primacy of parental influence over their child's development is being increasingly challenged by a variety of sources.

Growing attention is being paid to the *community effect*, the idea that a child's behaviour and aspirations are directly shaped by the community that she grows up in. Jencks and Mayer's analysis divides the community effect into four categories:

- *contagion/epidemic* – communities have a dominant set of social norms, that impact positively or negatively on pupil norms.
- *collective socialisation* – all adults exert an influence on children as role models and enforcers of codes.
- *institutional* – there is a huge variation in the treatments given and opportunities offered to children in different neighbourhoods from institutions such as schools and the police force.

- *relative deprivation* – a child's academic and vocational expectations are shaped by the achievements of those around her.

Their review concludes that 'growing up in a high SES neighbourhood raises a teenager's expected educational achievement, even when the teenager's own family characteristics are the same.' (Jencks & Mayer, 1990). Neighbourhoods with a social mix appear particularly important for children from low SES families.

Peer group effects

Running alongside the community effect is the peer group effect, the influence of a child's peers (in both school and neighbourhood) on his academic and social development. The importance of the peer group effect on school performance is accepted. It has been estimated that 70-75 per cent of the variation in the performance of secondary schools is due to pupil intake (Mortimore *et al*, 1994). The statement made previously about social mix applies equally to schools; children from more affluent families tend to achieve well wherever they go to school; the lower a family's SES, the more important it is that its children attend socially mixed schools (Feinstein, 1998).

A psychological exposition of this effect is contained in the recent controversial work of Judith Rich Harris. *The Nurture Assumption* argues not that nurture is insignificant, but that a far higher proportion of that nurture is influenced by a child's peers than is normally assumed (Harris, 1998).

Harris describes the group socialisation theory. A child's peer group cannot be defined as a whole class, school or neighbourhood, but the small number of children that each child selects to be friends. It is this friendship group that Harris asserts has a huge influence over pupil achievement.

This view is radical, but, like the community effect in general, does not negate the influence of parents. Children have virtually no control over the neighbourhood they live in, only slightly more influence over the school they attend, and somewhat more say over the peer group they socialise in. A child's parents have chosen the community, the school and, to a large extent therefore, the sphere within which a child can choose his friends (although clearly the choices of some parents are more limited than those of others). What is striking about Harris' study is that, even within a school, children tend to gravitate to friendship groups of similar family SES. Supervision levels in the home may have less impact on child outcomes than supervision levels outside the home (in the school and neighbourhood), but the nature of what takes place outside the home has largely been determined by parental decisions and circumstances.

The influence of parental support for schools on school effectiveness

Attempts to unravel the 'school effect', the extent to which a school's quality can affect pupil achievement, continue unabated. Two common strands emerge. One is that family factors account for most of the variance in the educational performance of schools. In other words, the biggest influence a parent exerts over schools is when choosing a school. The other is that, within this paradigm, schools do matter, whatever intake they are working with (Mortimore & Whitty, 1997).

In this debate, separate attention has been given to the 'parent effect' on schools – the impact that parents have above and beyond the influence they have over their own children's learning. Although the quality of relationships between parents and schools is even more difficult to measure than parental involvement in their own children's learning, there is a sustained and growing belief amongst practitioners and policy makers that a 'positive home-school partnership' is a key factor to school effectiveness (Mortimore 1988; Sammons et al 1995). This view is shared by Ofsted, and is reinforced by evidence from large scale, cross-phase studies in the UK, Australia and the US (Brighouse & Tomlinson, 1991; Ofsted, 1995a; Ofsted, 2000). As the introduction discussed, the meaning of 'partnership' is problematic.

The parent effect appears equally important in schools across the range of situations. According to Ofsted reports, all of the designated Beacon Schools in the UK have good relationships with parents, and most of the two hundred schools under special measures in 1998 had weak relationships with the families of their pupils (Times Education Supplement, 3.4.98). A common factor in schools that have removed themselves from Special Measures is the involvement of parents in developing and supporting an action plan (Gray, 2000). The National Commission on Education's report on successful schools in disadvantaged areas noted that all these schools saw parents as 'co-educators and co-learners' (National Commission on Education, 1993). This is backed up by American research on 366 'myth-buster' schools (schools delivering above average results in poor areas), which found a common emphasis on parental involvement (*Times Education Supplement*, 21.5.99). A recent study of successful UK multi-ethnic schools also found that all these schools 'listened to and learnt from the students and their parents.' (Blair & Bourne, 1998).[1]

Given the wealth of research, inspection and anecdotal evidence, it may be pertinent to ask whether a school can be effective without policies that successfully engage parents, both in the school itself or in their individual child's school learning. At the same time, it is worth remembering Nechyba's assertion that 'parents who become involved in their children's school...are likely to differ in various unobserved ways from other parents, a fact that would cause us to overestimate parental impact on schools.' (Nechyba *et al*, 1999: 59). In other words, the greatest influence that 'involved' parents have on school effectiveness may be their home-based input with their children, rather than their school-based involvement. If this is the case, it might be more efficient for a school to prioritise attracting certain types of parents over involving reluctant parents. It could be argued that, within the education market place, this is already happening.

School-based parental support: who benefits?

There are debates over who benefits most from policies to engage parents in school life; the school itself, or the families that choose to become involved in the life of a school. Research has contested that the private benefits of parental involvement outweigh the public benefits, for instance the 'competent children' study in New Zealand, and McMillan's recent US study (McMillan, 1999; Wylie & Thomson, 1999). This may appear irrelevant; engaging parents in the life of a school can be a win-win situation for both school and pupil. However, in micro and macro policy terms, policies that encourage school-based involvement may have unintended distributional consequences. For instance, a parent who volunteers to spend time in his child's class may, intentionally or not, divert teacher time and resources to his child. Although parental involvement in school life can benefit a whole school, the welcoming of certain kinds of parents may alter school culture in a way that disadvantages the children of the uninvolved.

This has serious equity implications when one considers that, unlike home-based parental involvement, school-based involvement is finite; projects designed to encourage such active engagement could never accommodate the parents of every pupil. Even 'workshop' activities have finite benefits, in that a surfeit of parental attendance would dilute the time and resource inputs available. Although this may be changing, anecdotal evidence hints that school-based involvement has traditionally been dominated by parents of higher socio-economic status. There are many reasons why lower SES parents may be less involved in their child's school: their own school experiences may mean that they place less value on education; schools themselves may be structured to welcome middle class parents; and certain parents may lack the confidence and cultural capital that those (teachers) who encourage such involvement assume. School-based involvement needs to be carefully targeted if such activity is not to become a driver of further educational inequalities.

Conclusion

> Once children have started school, the level of parental interest in the child's education is an important factor. However, for school age children, even allowing for all these facts, children from lower income families do less well. (HM Treasury, 1999: 29)

Proving what appears obvious, that parents do matter, is often more difficult than challenging assumptions. Much work remains to be done in order to uncover the causal channels that determine pupil achievement. However, although the evidence base beyond the pre-school years is less secure than policy makers may assume, there is still good cause to agree that policies which successfully encourage parental involvement in pupils' learning and in school life will contribute to the general raising of achievement. This may already have occurred; the improvements in National Curriculum Assessment results, GSCE results and post-16 and post-18 staying-on rates, may partly be explained by the generally raised parental awareness of the importance of supporting their child's learning.

The evidence becomes more problematic if the policy ambition is to redress equality of opportunities or reduce inequalities of educational outcomes between different pupils and different schools. Whether or not parental involvement is, as Lake asserts, 'the main source of differences amongst children', the new access points between parents and schools that have opened up in the last thirty years have probably been a factor in increased educational inequalities (Lake, 1995). Certainly, small-scale targeted projects show that engaging parents can be a key protective barrier against socio-economic conditions that can breed underachievement. Yet in its current condition, parental involvement in children's learning is normally less of a protective barrier than a lever to maximise the potential of the already advantaged.

Even if the importance of parental involvement is taken as a fact, this poses as many questions as it answers. A strong parental interest and home-based involvement can compensate for the inadequacies of the most ineffective school. A child can, with family or individual effort, achieve his potential in spite of his school. Yet is the reverse also true? Can a child achieve his potential unless his parent is a partner in his learning? If schools become increasingly structured to rely on parental involvement in every child's learning, then are schools simultaneously structured to reinforce existing inequalities in levels of parental involvement? Such involvement is certainly distinct, and difficult to replicate in the school setting. Is it irreplaceable? A key question needs to be answered: can the education service be structured to enable as many children as possible can achieve their potential, whether assisted or hindered by their family situation?

Endnote

1   The case studies revealed a number of concerns held by the parents of students in multi-ethnic schools. Among them were 'problems about poor communication, lack of understanding and missed opportunities for effective partnership between parents and schools.'

2. Changing family and school contexts

Policies cannot be built on evidence alone. Policy formulation lags behind evidence, which itself is being lapped by the pace of changes in society. Expectations of families and schools need to be located in realistic current and future contexts. Education policies appear to be constantly catching up with societal shifts, and normally missing the mark. However, the structures that underpin families have evolved so rapidly that, if schools have been slow to adjust to these transformations, they are hardly unique amongst institutions, both public and private. The information provided below concentrates on changes that most affect home-school relationships; each section concludes with the possible implications of these changes on future policy and practice.

Changing families[1]

Box 2.1 Changing family patterns

A rising number of households have no children

56 per cent of households are childless, a rise from 45 per cent in 1971. Half of these households are one-person.

Families are becoming smaller

The average number of children born per woman in the UK has fallen to 1.73 children per woman, although its decline has abated in the last few years.

More children are being born outside marriage

Almost four in ten children are now born outside marriage, a four-fold rise since 1974. However, four fifths of births outside marriage are jointly registered by both parents.

More children are growing up with one resident parent

80 per cent of dependent children live in a family with two parents, compared to 90 per cent in 1972. Twenty-one per cent of mothers are lone mothers, up from 12 per cent in 1979.

More children are experiencing family breakdown

28 per cent of children experience family breakdown before the age of 16, double the rate in the 1970s. Stepfamilies with dependent children account for eight per cent of all families.

Family structures are becoming more fluid

Children are increasingly likely to experience living in a variety of types of families and households (Haskey, 1998). More children have a larger number of 'part-time parents' who influence their lives, from changing partners of a parent, to friendship groups, to extended family members, to paid help (Wilkinson, 2000).

> **Box 2.2 Changing employment and income patterns**
>
> *More women are in paid employment*
>
> Women now make up 44.8 per cent of the total workforce, a rise of 9 per cent since 1971, though the proportion has remained steady since 1993.
>
> *More mothers are in paid employment*
>
> The fastest growth in employment rates is occurring amongst mothers of children under five (Wilkinson, 2000).
>
> Full-time employment rate amongst mothers rose from 17 per cent to 26 per cent between 1984 and 1999, faster than among other women (Brannen *et al*, 1996).
>
> *Parents in employment are working longer hours*
>
> In 1988 fathers were working an average of 45.7 hours per week. A decade later they were working 47.3 hours per week. Mothers were working on average 27 hours per week in 1988. In 1998 this figure had increased to 32.6 hours, a rise of 5.6 hours (Labour Force Survey, 1998).
>
> One in four fathers are working more than 50 hours per week and nearly one in ten are working 60 hours or more per week. The proportion of mothers working more than 40 hours per week has risen dramatically, from 19 per cent in 1988 to 33 per cent in 1998 (Labour Force Survey, 1998).
>
> *Employment patterns are becoming more flexible*
>
> 40 per cent of the entire workforce is now in non-traditional, flexible employment (DfEE, 1999a).
>
> 38 per cent of mothers and 2 per cent of fathers are in part time employment (European Commission figures, in Burgess, 1998).
>
> Over the last 15 years much of the growth in employment has been in either long or short hours jobs, with a declining share offering a 'standard' working week.
>
> In a quarter of two parent households at least one parent works regularly in the evenings (Harkness, 1999).
>
> *The numbers of children who are growing up in families on low incomes or with no earner has increased significantly*
>
> One third of children live in households with less than half the average income, the highest level in Europe, and almost three and a half times the number in 1979 (HM Treasury, 1999).
>
> Eighty per cent of poor children live in a household which is not fully employed, and more than 50 per cent live in entirely workless households (HM Treasury, 1999).

Policy and practice implications

The previous chapter has already summarised how these statistics are relevant to educational achievement. It is worth noting that while the changes described above have been taking place, educational performance, as measured by crude attainment, has been rising. Whether or not the educational health of the nation is in decline, it would be difficult to pin the praise or blame for Britain's current educational performance on the erosion of traditional family and employment structures.

However, these changes are having a huge impact on the context in which home-school relations are framed:

- The locations that schools serve have an increasing proportion of households who are either without children, or who send their children to a school outside the locality.

- More than two decades of rising material inequalities between families are continuing to increase inequalities in the learning resources of children from birth onwards.

- In an increasing number of families, there is no single main adult contact between home and school, or that contact may not be a child's parent.

- Schools are catering for an ever-diversifying range of family structures and situations.

- During the past two decades, schools have been teaching an increasing number of children whose home lives range from being temporarily disrupted to in near-permanent crisis.

- An increasing percentage of potential support for schools and learning is paternal.

Changing parent-child relationships

Changing amount of time spent together

> The time parents have available for their children has been squeezed by the rapid shift of mothers into the paid labour force, by escalating divorce rates and the abandonment of children by their fathers, and by an increase in the number of hours required on the job. (UNICEF, 1993: 2).

US and UK data has shown that 'Total Contact Time' with children has dropped 40 per cent, or ten to twelve hours per week during the last quarter of a century (UNICEF, 1993). What these statistics do not reveal is how parents are spending their contact time. It may be, for instance, that parents are using their reduced time more productively, at least in the educational sense.

Changing gender roles

Although it may be instinctive to believe that fathers are now more involved in raising their children, research has generally shown this shift to be exaggerated (Burgess, 1998). Paternal involvement in the early years has undoubtedly increased, but is often not sustained. For instance, only 1.7 per cent of fathers have become full time carers while their partners work full time, although there is evidence that many unemployed men are sharing childcare as never before (Sly, 1994).[2]

In single parent families, or after family breakdown, the picture for paternal involvement is mixed. Statistics reveal that:

- three per cent of fathers never see their child
- 47 per cent of fathers see their children at least weekly
- six per cent of fathers have 'shared residence' (at least one third of the time)
- 75 per cent of UK fathers are still in touch with their children five to ten years after separation (Burgess, 1997).

Changing conceptions of children's and parents' rights

This may be the most important factor in the changing relationship between parents and their children. Recent rulings and legislation, particularly the 1989 Children Act, have legislated for a clear ideological shift towards giving children rights on their own behalf (Lansdown, 1995). The 1999 Human Rights Act will maintain this momentum, giving children direct access to rights and freedoms guaranteed under the ECHR and UK law.

The cliché that 'children know their rights only too well' may be rooted in false nostalgia, but there can be little doubt that adult authority has to be justified as never before. Respect still exists, but now has to be earned. More than ever, children have the legal and societal weight to challenge parental authority.

The changing influences on children

Even if decreasing contact time and increasing children's rights have not led to the waning of parental influence on children, other forces may have. Technological changes and other social forces mean that children have access to an increasing variety of information sources, all of which may erode the influence, educational or otherwise, of parents. In a recent survey, 20 per cent of the parents said that television had more influence than they did on their children (McCarraher, 1998).

In contrast, growing fears over children's out-of-home safety (fears unsupported by statistics) have reduced most children's personal space (Mental Health Foundation Study, 1999). Parents may have less time for children, but it is likely that the time available is being spent with or very near them. This may actually be reducing other influences, such as peer group or community effects.

Changing attitudes to parenting

Economic and social forces described above appear to have created a widening range of parenting strategies, a range that has probably increased material and emotional inequalities between different children.

On the one side, there is evidence that pressure to be a 'perfect parent' is growing, to the extent that many parents are becoming increasingly proactive in the planning of their children's lives. At the extreme end there is the trend for 'teaching' your unborn child through prenatal exercises such as talking through some simple sums. Many parents are moving in the 'hyper-parenting' direction, aided by ever improving information and resources. Those with the capital to make such choices about parenting, whether that involves determining a child's diet, leisure activities, or educational input, can attempt to maximise existing advantages as never before.

On the other, reported cases of children at risk, especially in the category of 'neglect', have risen during the last two decades. There has also been a significant increase in the numbers of children starting school or pre-school with speech and language difficulties (AFASIC research in The Independent, 16.5.96).

These differences may partly be explained by the three-decade growth in prosperity and poverty, and the differential hierarchy of needs that this produces. This explanation is dangerous, since it implies that lower SES parents are less interested in their children's well being and education. Many empirical studies have shown this not to be the case (Tomlinson, 1991). Another theory is that as parenthood is increasingly professionalised through the use of agencies, particularly in low SES areas, parents feel disempowered from the parenting process and thus surrender responsibilities to the caring professions.[3]

Policy and practice implications

The mantra 'parents are a child's first and enduring educators', seems true to the point of banality, yet is also being challenged by a plethora of societal shifts. The liberation of access to information through new technologies, new forms of socialisation and the growing attention to children's rights, all have the potential to undermine the traditional primacy of parental influence. Psychologically, parenting appears to be more difficult than ever, while some of the very sources of these difficulties, within Government, Industry and the Media, are applying increasing pressures and support to be a 'perfect parent' (and, indeed, a 'perfect child'). For schools, changes in parent-child relationships mean:

- Although enthusiasm may be increasing, opportunities for parental support for a child's learning and school are being squeezed by time pressures, mainly work-related.

- In terms of gender, changing parenting patterns have not kept pace with changing employment patterns. By targeting paternal involvement in learning, schools could have a key role in moving families towards greater gender equality in childcare.

- Schools also need to target home-school links towards non-resident fathers, some of whom may find the school an ideal place for renewed contact.

- Parental involvement strategies may prove a huge waste of energy unless children are willing partners in the process.

- Schools are facing a wider variety of parenting strategies at all stages, including children who may be over or under-parented. In practice, some parents rely on schools for most of a child's education and socialisation; for others, attendance at school is a small part of a child's organised learning programme.

Changing family-school relationships

As well as the family changes described above, there are also broader themes, unrelated to family changes, that impact on home-school relationships. This section surveys the roles, responsibilities and attitudes of families and schools.

Roles and responsibilities

Defining obligations

A comparison between schools' and parents' legal obligations to children's learning is fascinating. The statutory requirements that schools have to parents have grown considerably. These include:

- The obligation to provide parents with a variety of information about the school and about their individual child (see chapter 3).

- The obligation to provide clear admissions procedures, and to enrol any child unless the school's rolls are full.

- The obligation to enter children for National Curriculum Assessment Tests, unless a parent chooses to withdraw a child.

- Child protection obligations.

- The obligation to inform a parent if a child is excluded; the DfEE has also advised schools to notify parents on the first day of non-attendance (DfEE Circular, 10/99).

Parents have basic duties related to the social development of their children. However, the legal obligations of parents to their children's learning or school has remained unchanged since the 1944 Education Act. Unless a parent is educating his child at home, his duties consist of making sure that his child attends a school, arrives on time and, if necessary, is collected at the end of the day. Any other involvement with the child's learning or school is done on a voluntary basis. The new Parenting Orders, which offer support, pressure and ultimately prosecution for the parents of persistent truants, merely reinforce this existing obligation.

This report does not recommend any increase in parents' statutory obligations,. However, if this it is to remain a constant, then it follows that *any further compulsory initiatives on schools towards parents will further tip this balance of obligations towards schools and teachers. This consideration informs all of the policy recommendations in this report.*

Defining roles

Fixed obligations tell a small part of the home-school story, as every school and virtually every parent in the country go beyond these obligations. Consensus exists that the boundaries between the educational roles of families and schools have become increasingly blurred. The best example of this synthesis is found in an exploration of the school and 'out of school' curriculum. Schools are now expected to teach children a range of topics, both within and beyond the National Curriculum, that might previously have been seen as impinging on parents' roles as educators: sex, drugs and parenting education, as well as out of hours learning activities such as homework clubs. At the same time, schools are becoming increasingly reliant on parents to assist their children through core and other areas of the curriculum, especially when national tests loom. This is a major issue for family-school relationships; the quantity of what parents and schools do for children has increased, but has the quality and consistency?

Home-school agreements

The source of this idea was undoubtedly bottom-up, and the use of home-school contracts increased organically during the 1990s (RSA/NAHT, 1992). Home-school agreements were introduced into all schools in England in September 1999. The agreements are not legally binding or actionable through courts. Children cannot be refused admission if their parents do not sign the agreement (DfEE, 1998a).

HSAs will therefore not shift the balance of statutory obligations between parents and schools. Concerns still exist that, even in their current form, HSAs may promote a rigid concept of 'good parenting', or initiate a litigation culture between schools and parents (Blair & Waddington, 1997). Yet they could also serve to clarify precisely what families and schools expect of each other. In Citizenship terms, HSAs are placed within a framework of civic responsibilities and generation of social capital, an important change from the consumer rights model espoused in the Parents' Charters.

It is too early to judge their impact. DfEE Guidance on HSAs is clear that the process is as important, if not more so, than the product (DfEE, 1998a). There is plenty of evidence of best practice, yet this may be outweighed by the low levels of consultation in many schools (Ouston & Hood 2000; ACE Bulletin 89). This could be due to workload and time pressures, perceived or actual lack of parental interest.

DfEE guidance states that 'agreements will work best when they are agreed and not imposed [by schools on parents]' (DfEE, 1998a). Ironically, it may be the Government's compulsory imposition of HSAs on schools that reduces their potential effectiveness. HSAs became another initiative to tick off during what was, by all accounts, a busy year for initiatives. If this is the case, it could serve as a warning for other home school initiatives. *Voluntarism should be the default option for national home-school initiatives – if in doubt, avoid the statutory.* The key role for national government is to offer guidance, support and expectations to encourage home-school links.

Parents' attitudes and opinions

Parents' views of schools

Attempts to homogenise parents' views have always been awkward, and the increasing family diversity described above makes this more so. Beyond basic expectations for children's literacy, numeracy and happiness, it is impossible to identify a shared set of parental beliefs and assumptions. However, there are attitudinal shifts, which are influencing client-professional relationships across all services. These are worth exploring in the family-school context.

In all public services there is a front line perception that users now show decreasing deference to institutions and their employees, especially in the public sector. To summarise, the assumptions are that the following social forces:

- increased levels of education for the majority of the population
- improved access to information that was previously retained by the 'professional'
- a societal trend to question professional authority and 'expert systems'
- deliberate public service transparency and responsiveness, opening up professional authority to scrutiny
- more private sector 'opt out' choices, and more people with the resources to make this decision

Have had the following aggregate effects:

- rising expectations of what the public sector should deliver
- increased awareness of rights, and willingness to express them
- increasing demands from clients for closer, more embedded relationships with public services

The social forces described undoubtedly apply to the education service, although there has been no increase in the proportion of children educated privately for over a decade. Yet have these forces delivered the assumed effects?

Are parents' expectations of schools rising?
Parents' expectations of the breadth and quality of what schools should achieve appear to be rising with those of successive governments, yet at a different pace and with different priorities.

Parental views of school *quality* are, generally, far more positive than the views of governments or other education stakeholders. In the most recent of many surveys, nine out of ten parents with children at state schools say they are happy with the quality of education, with even inner city secondary schools scoring highly.[4] Although there are concerns about general school standards, Michael Barber has written that many parents are 'alarmingly happy' about the schools their children attend (Barber, 1994). Ofsted data has revealed that dissatisfaction with standards of achievement is uncommon, and that anyway 'standards are not a priority'.[5] To Ofsted and the Government's dismay, parents are often highly satisfied with schools that have been deemed as failing, and highly involved in campaigning to prevent the closures of these schools.

Parental views of school *function* are diffuse, and are diversifying in tandem with the widening attitudes to their own educational role. The National Curriculum is broadly supported, as is national testing, although there have been recent concerns about the stress of primary tests. If anything, parents are more conservative than governments or schools. Many of the new demands placed on schools, for instance the offering of support services described in chapter 5 have not occurred as a result of parental pressure.

Are more parents willing to express their rights, or those of their children?
The brief answer to this question is 'not yet', although evidence is lacking since schools are not yet obliged to have an official complaints procedure. At the extremes, there are some pointers:

- The number of appeals against school admissions has risen dramatically (see chapter 7).

- Reported and unreported assaults by parents on teachers appears to be rising, according to teachers' associations (NAHT survey, 2000; Teacher line survey, 2000).

- There are predictions that an increasing number of parents will be willing to sue schools or local education authorities if their children's schooling has been unsatisfactory.

Yet all of these instances involve a minority of parents. In spite of the fact that many parents now have more letters after their name than their child's teacher, and in spite of the media-fuelled decline in the status of teachers, it appears that compliance is still the norm. It is difficult to surmise whether this compliance is built on trust or deference. Crozier argues that 'Working class parents tend to be more deferential towards the professionalism of teachers, appearing at times to take a fatalistic view of their children's education' (Crozier, 1997: 197). Although there are clearly class differentials in the parent-school relationship, the feeling of parental powerlessness may actually be the norm. Parents may talk disparagingly of schools and teachers outside the school building, yet it is almost a case of 'no assertiveness beyond this line' for most parents.

One group who may be gaining in confidence are minority ethnic parents. Again, these parents are anything but homogenous, but some generalisations can be drawn. Minority ethnic parents have always placed high value on their children's education and with time have become increasingly participatory in their children's schools and schooling (Runneymede Trust, 1998; Dosanjh & Ghuman, 1997). The renewed attention and resources given to ethnic minority achievement and the combating of racism in schools may give minority ethnic parents the confidence and armoury to be more proactive when their child's schooling is unsatisfactory. This is a significant challenge and opportunity for schools.

Generally, however, parental expression of rights is limited. Most of this is channelled into choice of schools; indeed, school choice may have become a convenient valve through which parental dissatisfaction about schools is safely released.

Are views of relationships changing?

Parental views on their relationships with their child's learning and school will be considered throughout the rest of this report. Two initial generalisations can be drawn. One is that parental acceptance and enthusiasm for supporting their child's learning is greater than the enthusiasm for supporting their child's school. The other, borne out especially by the research on schools' self evaluation, is that in answering 'what makes a good school?' parents give a higher priority to home-school links than do teachers or pupils (MacBeth, 1999).

As well as parents who do not desire such links, there are undoubtedly many parents who find it difficult to access such relationships. This has a class dimension. Although research repeatedly shows that parents of all social groups have an interest in helping with their children's education, studies have also revealed that working class parents in particular find it difficult to establish a productive relationship with their children's schools (Rutter & Madge, 1976;

Hannon, 1995; Weinberger, 1996; ATD Fourth World, 2000). In addition, there is a significant minority of parents who are profoundly disaffected from an education system that has probably failed them, and is likely to be failing their children.

Schools' views of parents

As with parents, there is a spectrum of teacher attitudes to and expectations of parents, both between and within schools. Although they may be generalisations, two important strands can be drawn from current research. One is that teachers have recognised the importance of parental engagement in a child's learning (if not school) on a child's achievement as an embedded but possibly irreplaceable influence. Teachers' expectations of the quantity and quality of parental input into their children's formal learning has undoubtedly risen. The other strand is that many schools and teachers apply a negative 'deficit perspective' view of parents who do not offer overt support, or whose parenting skills are seen to be more generally lacking. A consequence of this pathological analysis may be that teachers have lower expectations of pupils with 'uninterested parents' (Apple & Zenk, 1996).

Research suggests that many teachers are more sceptical about investing energy in improving home-school links. A pre-election survey of teachers found that, within New Labour's manifesto, 'the stress on parental involvement [in schools] was particularly resented' (RSL/TES survey, 1997). Why is this the case? One cause must be the increased time constraints and externally imposed pressures on schools. Another is the lack of attention given to parents during teachers' initial teacher training and continuing professional development. Another important factor appears to be how home-school links might threaten power relations between teachers and parents.

Children's views of family-school relationships

Children are rarely asked their views on parental involvement. The only recent UK study has found that children have clear views about home-school relations and about the separation between home and school (Edwards *et al*, 2000). They can be active in supporting or resisting parental involvement or uninvolvement. The study is also revealing race, class and gender differentials in views of involvement; in particular, boys from working class backgrounds are active in resisting parental involvement and are keen to maintain the home-school boundaries.

Policy and practice implications

Implications are more difficult to draw from the qualitative research summarised above.

- Although there is acceptance from both parents and teachers that their educational influences are embedded and difficult to unmesh, role confusion undoubtedly acts as a barrier to quality home-school relationships. Asking teachers to be parents and parents to be teachers is also a major cause of overload for parents, teachers and especially children. For this reason, the opportunity costs of any initiative described in this report must be seriously evaluated.

- The expectations that families and schools have of each other have diversified. Rigid legislation designed to improve home-school relationships may become increasingly fruitless. Voluntarism should be the default option for national home-school initiatives – if in doubt, avoid the statutory.

- Intervention to improve home-school relationships needs to be targeted, if such improvement is not to be a driver of further educational inequalities.

- Schools need to consult closely with their pupils over home-school initiatives and policies. Schools need to work with the fact that many pupils value the separation between their home and school lives.

Relationships within the trinity of parent, teacher and child have become increasingly complex, but the boundaries between professional and parent appear surprisingly stable. Reasons for this situation are explored throughout this report, yet its underlying thesis is this; in spite of the political, social, and economic developments described thus far, the cultures of most schools in relation to their links with parents have remained relatively static. This intransigence may be short lived. Many of these forces, in particular the impact of new technologies and the growth of litigation culture, have their own momentum that is likely to change home-school relationships. Schools may have a limited time within which to shape their futures.

Endnotes

1. Unless stated, statistics come from Family Policy Studies Centre (2000).
2. According to the Carlton Fathers pamphlet, 'no more than one in every 100 two-parent families contain a true househusband.'
3. For a wider discussion on how separation of work and leisure and the expertise of scientists/specialists have turned the family into a leisure service, whose main purpose is entertainment, see Zeldin T (1995), and Hardyment C (1983).

4   In an ICM poll of parents 91 per cent of parents were happy with the quality of their children's schools, reported in *The Guardian* (29.2.00). See also Edexcel, 2000.
5   Reported in the *Times Educational Supplement* (9.10.98) and taken from an unpublished OFSTED report finding that 'most parents are very supportive of their child's school. Where there was dissatisfaction no link was found to quality of education.'
6   The Runnymede Trust (1998) report provides strategies for all adults who influence the educational experience of young children.

II: Family and School as Mutual Support Mechanisms

3. Home-school communication

Education and other public services require a far more interactive relationship between client and provider. (IPPR, 1991: 36)

Effective two-way communication is arguably the most important but least measurable factor in developing successful home-school relationships. Every initiative described throughout this report takes this as a given quality. Many variables come into play, from the 'professional mindset' of teachers, to the (less discussed) 'parental mindset' to the fabric of the built environment (as a teacher, my most positive year of home-school communication was purely because my classroom was on the ground floor, with a door to the playground). As with so many other professional-client relationships in public and private institutions, what schools call 'communication' often stretches no further than the transmission of information, and schools with excellent communication strategies still rarely reach all parents.

In recent decades, in many schools and with most families, home-school communication appears to be gradually moving from a problem-based last-resort norm to a more constant constructive dialogue. Yet there is still a long way to go, and school-to-home communication seems to be further along this axis than home-to-school. In 1988, researching parental involvement in Europe, Macbeth asked 'what are the psychological implications of parent-teacher contact tending to be only at times of crisis?' (Macbeth, 1989). This question is still pertinent. In the ATL/IPPR survey (see appendix), 41 per cent of primary teachers and 66 per cent of secondary teachers agreed that most of their interactions with parents were to resolve problem situations.

Recent legislation, that will be discussed below, has placed the onus on schools to maximise their communication to (not with) parents. Schools may need to refocus their attentions, in spite of sustained demands for ever-more information, to optimise rather than maximise their communication mechanisms. This is especially relevant in the new information age; as printing costs lower and websites permit virtually unlimited space, schools need greater levels of self-editing as a bulwark against information overload.

The structures that schools create in order to communicate with parents also ask some resonant efficiency and equity questions. Put simply, these questions are:

- How can schools and parents communicate necessary information whilst avoiding a counter-productive overload?
- How can schools ensure that their communication mechanisms are equally accessible to all parents, regardless of home factors?

These are issues that all public services are currently grappling with. Research outlined in the 'Modernising Government' White Paper reveals that citizens feel, relative to other services, well informed about their schools (Cabinet Office, 1999). However, in the 'people's panel' commissioned by the Cabinet Office, twelve per cent said that educational institutions either provide only limited amounts of information or do not tell them much at all (Cabinet Office, 1998).

Modes of communication

Schools and parents interact through (mainly nationally imposed) formal mechanisms and (self-generated) informal 'bridges', conveying both information about the school and about individual pupils' progress. Figure 1 maps communication onto these categories, although a feature of schools with effective communication strategies may be that the formal and informal are often barely distinguishable. This chapter will discuss the issues that relate to communication on an individual basis. Communication with parents as groups will be covered in later chapters.

Table 3.1 Communication

	Formal mechanisms	*Informal 'bridges'*
About school	Open meetings for learning support Governors' annual report and annual parents' meeting PTAs and other structures Prospectuses League Tables/SAT performances Inspection reports Class meetings	Newsletters Open days Noticeboards Websites Social events School handbooks Media publicity
About individual progress	Progress reviews (parents evenings and alternatives) Pupil reports End of Key Stage assessments Target setting Home visits	Phone calls/emails Chance or arranged meetings Homework-related feedback Home-school diaries

Communication about the school

Schools' legal requirements to provide information about themselves to parents and others have increased enormously. This was centrally driven by a market philosophy, a rights-based desire for 'parent power' through information, and an often neglected wish for schools to define and describe their individual ethos. The 1991 Parent's Charter, updated in 1994, standardised schools' information obligations (DES, 1994). Parents were given the 'right to know' about their child's progress through an annual report, to include national test results. Yet the dominant aspect of the Parents' Charter concerned new obligations on schools to provide information about their institutional progress, not their individual pupils'. In effect, the 'right to know' was merely the information arm of the 'right to choose'. These requirements were, and still are, as follows:

- Regular inspection reports (see chapter 7)
- National Curriculum Assessment Tests and GCSE performance
- School prospectuses
- Governors' annual report and meeting (see chapter 7)

The quality of these outputs varies greatly between schools. A 1996 Consumers Association report found that 79 of 80 schools surveyed failed to give parents the information they were required to supply by law.[1] If this is still the case, it may be due to a mixture of unhealthy neglect and healthy resistance. There is little evidence as to whether these requirements were a response to parental demand. Research into parents' desires for information point to a hunger for details about their own child's progress, not more information about the school (CEDC, 1998). Schools could merely be prioritising the wishes of parents over legal obligations; certainly, many popular schools pay scant attention to, for instance, the governors' annual report.

However, there is no doubt that these documents are now embedded in the educational system. In spite of complaints about bureaucracy, the ATL/IPPR teachers' survey found opinion evenly divided on the statement that 'schools are required to give too much information to parents'. Many schools already offer additional open evenings to communicate with parents over a variety of issues, and also give information through newsletters and websites.

The list above will shortly be added to; the recent Freedom of Information Bill proposes more information rights for parents, including information on admissions policies and how other decisions are made (Home Office, 1999).

After this Act, *there should be a cessation of further imposed requirements on schools to publish generic information about themselves. In particular, pressure for schools to provide information to the DfEE of baseline assessments and Key Stage One tests for performance table purposes should be resisted.* Instead, schools should be encouraged to refocus their efforts on providing more honest, detailed and comprehensible information about individual pupils.

Communication about individual progress

When I received your note, I was trembling, even before I read it.
Message from a parent to a teacher

At best, communication about a pupil's progress should both stimulate and shape parental involvement in that pupil's learning. Such communication often occurs through the 'bridges' listed above. However, formal procedures are important for two reasons: first, the opportunities for informal contact are not necessarily equal for all parents. As the NCC/*Service First* report on home-school communication asserted, the absence of structures and procedures in schools can lead to a 'free for all', requiring parents to 'catch' a teacher at the end of the day favoured more assertive parents at the expense of less confident ones (National Consumer Council/Service First, 1997: 15). Second, opportunities for informal contact decline as pupils move through the education system.

The traditional, formal mechanisms that schools use to provide such information are oral progress reviews and written reports. Both are worthy of separate analysis, although, as best practice indicates, they are more effective when they form elements of an ongoing, continuous process.

Progress reviews

A cross between a social security office, Kings Cross Station and a doctor's surgery (Nias, 1981: 92).

Progress reviews are generally known as parents' evenings, although many schools are adapting to more flexible timing. Research concerning parents' evenings have produced overwhelmingly negative conclusions, although this is far less true for primary schools. Almost all parents interviewed for recent research in secondary schools found them 'a frustrating experience; and for many, deeply distressing.' (Walker, 1998: 168). As one mother said, 'there's plenty of potential for feeling totally inadequate.' (Walker, 1998: 170).

Many commentators have blamed this failing on professional capture of proceedings. Yet further research has shown that teachers appear to a large extent just as fearful and suspicious of and disempowered by parents' evenings. The research cited above argues that recent legislation 'may have contributed towards undermining teachers' confidence but appears to have done little to empower parents.... Identity was in jeopardy for all concerned' (Walker, 1998: 175). Bastiani sums up the evidence by describing evenings as 'a process which is characterised by mismatching expectations and mutual incomprehension.' (Bastiani, 1989).

In spite of this, attendance at parents' evenings is high, especially by mothers, and evenings appear to be increasing to a termly norm. The major issues are whether schools are maximising the value of such occasions. Among issues that schools need to consider are:

- *purpose* – parents need to be made aware of the precise reason for attending any meeting. For instance, many schools now use the autumn meeting as an information gathering exercise. If the meeting is to discuss a written document, this should be given to parents well in advance of any meeting. If two-way communication is desired, this needs to be made explicit.

- *timing* – 'progress reviews' should take place at flexible times, to accommodate for parents' different working patterns. End of year reviews are not especially effective at pre-empting problems at an early stage. For this and other reasons, schools should also develop structures for other meetings as and when necessary.

  For example, Rush Common Primary School in Oxfordshire has pioneered a system of 'parent surgeries' in place of conventional parents' evenings. Each class teacher is available one day a week to talk to parents after school has finished. This gives parents the chance to talk to teachers in greater depth than in the past and at any times during the year they feel in need of support.

- *repeat sessions* – schools need to recognise that, for various reasons, a pupil's parents may wish to see teachers separately. Currently, the norm is that a non-resident parent would need to ask for this 'favour'. Instead, this opportunity should be built into the invitation procedure.

- *setting* – there is no reason why meetings have to take place in the school. Given time and resources, such a meeting could occur through a home visit. Schools with low turnouts should explore the possibility of holding meetings in alternative locations, such as shops, libraries or community centres.

- *role of pupil* – many schools and parents are ambivalent about how pupils should be involved in meetings, or if they should be present at all. Schools need to develop their own policies regarding this (even if they decide that the decision should be left to the parent).

- *barriers to attendance* – a common complaint from teachers is that 'you never see the ones you need to see'. Schools should not resign themselves to this situation. Many schools now give fixed appointment times to all parents, regardless of whether they have responded to an invitation. Others use 'mopping up' procedures, and may offer free transport to school.

- *barriers to participation* – schools also need to offer appropriate support for those with limited English or low literacy levels. This is where an LEA could play a key support role, particularly if meetings are staggered between different schools.

- *honesty* – the accentuation of the positive can render meetings virtually useless. Honesty is more likely to be achieved if such a meeting is not an isolated event, but part of a deeper relationship.

- *preparation for teachers* – one teacher in the ATL/IPPR survey wrote that 'every NQT's nightmare is the first parents' evening'. Teachers need training to both raise their confidence and lower their professional guard.

At primary level, progress reviews can build on more informal, as-and-when communication. As these opportunities decrease at secondary school, the importance of formal occasions grows, yet parental attendance and satisfaction with progress reviews decline. The traditional secondary school parents evening needs an urgent overhaul, especially the pattern of trying to see every subject teacher. The case study below describes one alternative.

Box 3.1 Academic review days: a family-friendly alternative?

Academic review days are a key aspect of the Value-Added and Attainment Project, co-ordinated at London University's Institute of Education. The project has so far worked with twenty LEAs or consortia, 235 Schools and 8,000 teachers. Review days are offered as an alternative to traditional parents' evenings, the main differences being:

- The tutor has used information from subject teachers to gain a holistic picture of each student's progress.
- Information is clearer and more honest, with explicit individual targets, both academic and social.
- The teaching timetable is suspended for a day for timetabled meetings with parents. Evening appointments are also possible.
- The Year tutor is at the centre of the process, not the subject teachers. Parents have an interview with their child's personal tutor, who has gathered information from his subject teachers, and has a whole picture of the student. The aim to the meeting is to engage in 'a quality discussion about learning, which is seldom possible in the snatched moments with numerous teachers on traditional parents' evenings'.
- These build on termly one-to-one tutorial reviews between student and tutor.
- Parents are given clear and honest information about current attainment. This strategy is complemented by a new approach to reports, with clearer focus on understandable data, and less on narrative.
- Learning targets are set at the review, based on the ongoing formative value added approach. Advice is given on practical strategies that can enable the student to take 'the next steps'.
- Schools that have initiated academic review days have found a sustained increase in attendance. Parents have also been supportive of the fact that this is a more private process.

(Hodgson *et al*, 1998)

School reports

As late as the 1960s, the majority of school reports consisted of a list of test scores and class positions (Reid, 1984). There has been a universal shift to the current norm of more personalised reports, including requests for feedback. Yet whether this has made reports more 'user friendly', or merely replaced one form of jargon with another, more convoluted version, is open to question.

Ofsted's analysis of parent questionnaires argued that parents were in danger of information overload from reports, and that national curriculum-related comments were confusing (Ofsted, 1995b). A recent RISE survey of secondary school reporting systems, and parents' attitudes to them, found widespread dissatisfaction (Clark & Power, 1998). One recurring issue for parents was the fact that end of year reports were 'too late'. There was also a concern about computer-generated sentences, a 'widely expressed fear that the technology, rather than the teacher, controlled the content.' (Clark & Power, 1998: 35).

In many ways, the issues for schools to address are similar to those mentioned above regarding progress reviews. Again, reports should accommodate diverse family structures and language needs. Current initiatives to reduce the bureaucratic burdens on teachers may yield reporting systems that are more user friendly for both writer and reader (DfEE, 1998b). The *honesty* issue is crucial; the trend for 'positive reporting' has led to form letter style reporting, in the format of 'x can (add often vague national curriculum statement)'. Positive does not necessarily mean constructive. As one father argued in the RISE research: 'When they're not doing well I think it's actually better to say that they're not doing well as opposed to fudging the issue.' (Clark & Power, 1998).

National end of year assessments can, if used and explained appropriately, create a framework for more honest reporting. Yet such assessments can only be summative, and reports should aim to be formative. If they are to remain annual (and many schools are already reporting more frequently), *reports should be written halfway through the year, to give parents, pupils and teachers the time to work through the issues during the rest of the school year.*

Target setting

Target setting for individual children has gradually grown in use to become a widespread practice in schools. The agreement of termly targets through an Individual Education Plan, used for pupils with Special Educational Needs, is moving to the mainstream, and is being piloted for every child in some EAZs and 'Fresh Start' schools.[2] The DfEE Standards website's best practice guidance on target setting states that 'there must be effective communication with parents about the targets set and progress towards meeting them.' The Value Added and Achievement Project, cited above, is an excellent example of this. With the exception of a few secondary schools, target setting in schools is still at an embryonic stage – research is needed about how the process and product can impact on pupil, parent and teacher motivations.

Home visits

Home visits are used in many schools, particularly at transition points. They can be effective tools in initiating communication, particularly for those parents who, for various reasons, feel uncomfortable in the school setting. They can also give teachers a new understanding of a child's development and out of school life. For this reason, *space should be made for home visits as an integral part of every teacher's continuing professional development*. There are clear issues related to invasion of personal spaces – *home visits should never be obligatory, nor should they be a pre-requisite for admission*. Yet they also give the opportunity for parents to communicate with teachers in their space and on their terms (see Alexander *et al*, 1995).

Overarching issues and opportunities

Two-way communication

Much of the emphasis on improving home-school communication, whether at local or national level, has focussed on how schools can improve their communication *to* parents. Schools and other educational bodies need to evaluate existing procedures to establish how much of their communication strategy is one-way. Home-school diaries, for instance, may seem like an ideal channel for two-way communication. Yet research on literacy in primary schools claims that 'Most heads and post-holders seemed to see [them]…as part of their missionary work to parents, providing an opportunity to explain what the child had been doing and enlist parents' help in tackling any problems that had arisen, rather than as a communication between co-equal partners' (Wragg *et al*, 1998). As with so much communication, the attitude may be more important than the activity.

A good example of how this pattern can be reversed is through parental involvement in assessment. This has mainly been used in early years settings, and with SEN children through the Portage scheme (Wolfendale, 1995). However, there is no reason why such involvement should not extend to older age groups, as a valuable supplement to national assessments. Reviewing the evidence, Wolfendale concludes that 'the quality of content of parental input is equal to that of trained professionals' (Wolfendale, 1992). The existing target setting process can provide opportunities for parents to be involved in the assessment of their child.

If communication is unequally balanced, the blame for this should not only be directed at schools. If schools are to build relationships and raise the achievement levels of their students, it is often vital that they know about circumstances, positive or negative, that may be affecting their learning. These could include family changes, the receiving of private tuition or attendance at a supplementary school. Apart from medical information and the application procedures for certain schools, parents have no statutory duty to give any information about their children to their schools. Although it would be unjustifiable to oblige parents to communicate predicaments that they may wish to keep confidential, *there could undoubtedly be a mixture of pressure and support, possibly located at the national level, for parents to let schools know*. However, this would only be valuable if schools were then equipped with the will and resources to act on such information, and provide additional support where necessary.

Use of Information and Communications Technology

New and future developments in ICT carry obvious potential for home-school communication. Schools have been swift to develop websites as a means of transmitting generic information. Again, the focus has been on one–way communication, and most school websites are a long way from being truly interactive, but their quality is improving fast.[3] Further research needs to be carried out on how schools can exploit the online facilities to improve two-way communication with parents.

Schools are also beginning to harness ICT to develop new forms of communication regarding individual pupils. Creative use of ICT may eventually replace the annual or termly report with a more ongoing system of reporting a child's progress. At the same time, the widespread use of opaque computer-generated statement banks for reports, as cited above, should serve as a warning against the efficacy of some ICT 'shortcuts'.

Box 3.2 IBM – Reinventing education

Using IBM's *Wired for Learning*, these programmes aim to improve home-school communication through:

- Building conference software for threaded discussion groups between teachers and parents (in Ireland – Wired for Learning)
- Enabling parents to see their child's work online.
- Creating ongoing systems to report children's progress

Already used in Ireland, the US, Brazil and Italy, the project is now being piloted in England's Beacon Schools.

Increasingly sophisticated telephone systems also offer opportunities. Through the Bridge Project in the US, one hundred schools in seven states have furnished voice mailboxes for teachers to leave recorded messages for parents. An evaluation found that teachers communicated with an average of 15 parents per day, compared with 3 a day before the system was installed. It also revealed that 43 per cent of families checked the mailbox at least once a week (TES, 30.5.97). This is especially relevant to larger secondary schools.

Electronic communication is creeping up on schools, and presents both an opportunity and a threat. By the middle of 1999, 15 per cent of primary and 32 per cent of secondary teachers had a personal e-mail address (up from two per cent and nine per cent in 1998) (DfEE, 1999d). However, it is unclear how many of these were accessible to parents and pupils. As all schools go online by the end of 2001, should all teachers be accessible to parents (and pupils) through an e-mail address? The potential benefits are clear, as is the possibility of some parents overloading teachers with queries. Without a clear policy, e-mails are likely to become burdensome. *In consultation with parents, schools need to determine the circumstances when e-mail communication is useful and appropriate.*

Box 3.3 Bromcom – MyChildAtSchool.com

MyChildAtSchool.com is an Internet link for parents to access information relating to their child's progress via the school's administration system. Future elements in development for the system are information on homework assignments, email messaging between parents and teachers and the ability to pay for school supplies, books and educational software and hardware.

The system includes up-to-date information about attendance, behaviour and academic progress, enabling parents to take immediate appropriate action, rather than wait for a parents' evening. It also centralises information and reduces paperwork and bureaucracy for teachers.

Access is an obvious issue for ICT initiatives to confront. The distribution of home computers is becoming increasingly skewed towards middle class homes (TES, 22.1.99). This is likely to change, but until access is universal, which probably means at least until the end of this decade, schools need to consider the equity of online resources as communication tools. It is inevitable that such resources will benefit the already privileged; schools can alleviate this by opening access to their ICT equipment and by ensuring that other communication channels are not yet jettisoned. Schools also need to ensure that any reduction in traditional communication systems does not disadvantage those without the resources or skills to access such systems. Even with universal access, interactive digital television will provide inferior access, since it offers a 'walled garden' of options, and does not have the capabilities of home computers.

Consultation about communication

How can a school know if its communication mechanisms are effective? National surveys can never give a precise picture of the local needs of a school population.

Some schools have evaluated their communication through a collective review of documentation. Some schools use exit surveys at parents' evenings to consult on their efficacy. Although such consultation may seem a bureaucratic burden on all concerned, schools can often streamline their communication as a result. LEAs or EAZ Forums could facilitate such evaluations on behalf of several schools.

Communicating with the 'not yet reached'

> *If any school thinks it has completely cracked communication, it probably hasn't listened hard enough.* Home-school liaison worker, London.

It is misguided to imagine a fixed group of families whom, for various reasons, schools constantly fail to interact with. It is more accurate to consider that all parents have fluctuating interaction levels that can be raised or reduced by home and school factors. Individual parents can be totally remote from some schools, yet intimately involved with others. A good example of this is the way in which some African-Caribbean parents respond to a sense of alienation from mainstream schools by taking an active role in their children's supplementary schools. Targeting of under-reached groups can prove fruitful. For instance, North Manchester High School for Girls held coffee mornings specifically for Asian mothers, which improved the attendance of this group at all school events, both social and academic. Schools have also found that sustained focus on a few parents can create positive ripples. As Cambridgeshire's manual for parent partnerships asserts, 'staff time initially invested in just one or two families from less advantaged, disempowered backgrounds may be well spent, as word spreads to other families lacking confidence' (Cambridgeshire County Council, 1999: 17).

Although a mixture of innovative strategies and individual charisma can regenerate communication in any school, there will always be occasions when communication with individual families breaks down or never gets going. At this point, the existence of a neutral broker, possibly in the form of home-school link workers described in the concluding chapter, can be especially useful. Yet, to repeat a strand running throughout this report, failure to communicate with a pupil's parents should, as far as possible, not prejudice against that pupil's learning potential. This is a huge challenge that all schools face.

When things go wrong: establishing a complaints procedure

Any communication strategy must embrace worst case scenarios. Currently, at school level, parents now have a formal right to complain about exclusions, admissions,

> **Box 3.4 The Haringey parental outreach team**
>
> This team was established by the LEA in 1995, funded by the Home Office. Sixty per cent of Haringey's pupils come from an ethnic minority background, and forty per cent of these are refugees.
>
> One of the main motivations for starting the team was the perception that the induction of refugee parents into schools was generally poor. For these parents to be partners in their children's education, they needed to be introduced to the complexities of the British education system. They were being denied access to key information.
>
> A multi-ethnic, multidisciplinary team, it aims to promote the role of parents in education through the provision of information, advice, advocacy and training for parents from seven targeted communities: Afro-Caribbean, Bangladeshi, Congolese, Eritrean, Kurdish, Somali and Turkish.
>
> The team is linked to existing community organisations (including one supplementary school), in which weekly advice surgeries are run. This enables these groups to develop capacity and expertise in educational support matters. The team also encourages and assists the creation of community based Parents Associations. Representatives of organisations are part of the recruitment panel for workers, who speak the language of the community they serve.
>
> In addition, parents are seen on an individual basis, through home visits, surgeries and advice clinics in schools themselves. Liaison is also done with schools to improve their relationships with families via mediation. Advocacy work is also carried out on behalf of individual children.
>
> www.haringey.gov.uk

SEN issues, and when a parent believes that a school is failing to deliver any aspect of the National Curriculum or Religious Education.

Schools should be statutorily required to have a complaints procedure. The 1998 Schools Standards and Framework Act legislated for this, but this has not yet occurred. As more responsibility and funds move away from LEAs (and their ombudsman) and to schools, this becomes more important. A complaints procedure gives a new opportunity for individual parental voice, and for schools to learn from this voice. It may prevent more aggressive forms of complaints, and litigation – experiences in other services show that complainants are mainly looking for an apology only. As a formal system, it is more equitable than the 'open door' policies of many heads.

The RISE study of complaints procedures gives detailed information and models (RISE, 1997). However, two other options should be added to their proposals

- *The procedure should include opportunities for complaints from pupils.*

- *The procedure should be two-way.* Teachers should be able to use the procedure to make official complaints about parents. Sanctions against aggressive parents are often fairly random; such a procedure could make them more open. For instance, there are stories of parents who receive indefinite bans from a school building for one act of verbal aggression.

What can be done at national level?

The National Curriculum and other centralising measures, from National Curriculum Assessment Tests to literacy and numeracy strategies, have granted the DfEE opportunities to inform parents about exactly what their children are learning. The DfEE already produces an accompanying leaflet for parents relating to every aspect of their child's education. The newest development addressing this is called *Learning Journey*, a Learning Partnership for children, parents and teachers where the use of design is strongly emphasised to engage all parties and as a bulwark against jargon. This includes a Parent's 'Rough Guide' to the National Curriculum. *The Learning Journey* initiative should make it easier for all parents to understand the structure of what children are learning at school. Other national organisations and projects, in particular the Advisory Centre for Education's *Step by Step* project, also offer impartial advice and information.

In this mainly positive context, *Service First*'s view that 'much of the failure of schools to address communications with parents can be put down to a centralised education system and lack of resources' is worthy of consideration (National Consumer Council/Service First, 1997: 22). Schools do not appear to have become over-reliant on national leaflets to give parents information; the increase in websites and newsletters refutes this. A more salient point is that, from the evidence presented in this chapter, communication may be an area where best practice is currently being achieved in spite of, rather than because of, public policy. Schools may achieve success only by prioritising their values and the perceived needs of their clients over nationally imposed obligations.

Policy conclusions

There is no single strategy that can answer the two questions posed in the introduction. The overload issue for schools is more related to other communication pressures; perhaps a rule of thumb for any *school*'s communication should be that *communication with parents should come first*. All other information demands, whether from Ofsted, LEAs or the DfEE, should automatically be a lower priority (this is obviously easier said than done!).

As for equal access, this is more dependent on the atmosphere and culture of schools than the mechanisms described above, although all these can contribute. It may be worth learning from the SEN experience, that *formal* procedures have facilitated communication with parents. This is also an area where useful resource and project levers can be pulled at supra-school levels.

Apart from complaints procedures, all of the recommendations for schools are made as optional suggestions. *Schools should*:

- reconsider their scheduling of progress reviews and annual reports
- ensure that all communication mechanisms are available to non-resident parents or other carers. This would require keeping the addresses of all 'part time parents'
- build communication improvements into their Development Plans (although not necessarily through numerical targets)
- evaluate and consult on all communication structures to improve levels of two-way communication
- consider the use of home visits as an integral communication tool and as part of every teacher's continuing professional development. However, home visits should never be obligatory, nor should they be a pre-requisite for admission
- consult with parents and pupils to establish a two-way complaints procedure by 2005

At the supra-school level LEAs and voluntary organisations should:

- support schools in improving communication to parents at transition points
- support schools in communicating with parents with low literacy levels or limited English, particularly at progress reviews
- offer free transport for parents in disadvantaged areas to attend progress reviews

At the national level, the DfEE should:

- legislate for all schools to establish complaints procedures by 2005
- beyond this, add no further requirements to schools' current statutory information obligations
- work with the Department of Trade and Industry to explore options for statutory paid leave to allow parents to attend progress reviews
- give 'communication with parents' more time and status in Initial Teacher Training, Continuing Professional Development, the National Professional Qualification for Headship and any performance management and appraisal systems
- co-ordinate a campaign to encourage parents to inform their child's school about any changes in family or other circumstances

Further research is required on:

- how the target setting process and product can impact on pupil, parent and teacher motivations
- how schools can exploit the online facilities, including email, to improve two-way communication with parents
- the best ways that pupils whose parents cannot be encouraged to communicate with the school can, where necessary, be given compensatory time and resources.

Endnotes

1 Reported in *TES* (27.9.96). Philip Cullum, the association's manager, said the lack of progress over the past three years was 'disappointing', with the very worst schools virtually implying 'that parents were an unavoidable inconvenience rather than encouraging them to be more involved with their children's education'.

2 See, for instance, Newham EAZ (www.newham.gov.uk/EAZ) and the Islington Arts and Media School.

3 Advisory Centre for Education (1999) has some useful advice on school websites, as well as some examples of how not to do it! See also: Parents Information Network (www.pin.org.uk).

4. School-based support

Previous chapters have charted the legal rights and duties that families and schools have towards each other. Anything beyond this relationship, either with each other or with a child's learning, occurs through exhortation, pressure, support and good will. It requires above all a recognition that a child's potential as a learner, and a school's potential as a learning institution, can only be reached if home-school relationships go far deeper than the compulsory. This chapter will focus on voluntary support that schools and families can offer each other. The chart below categorises this support.

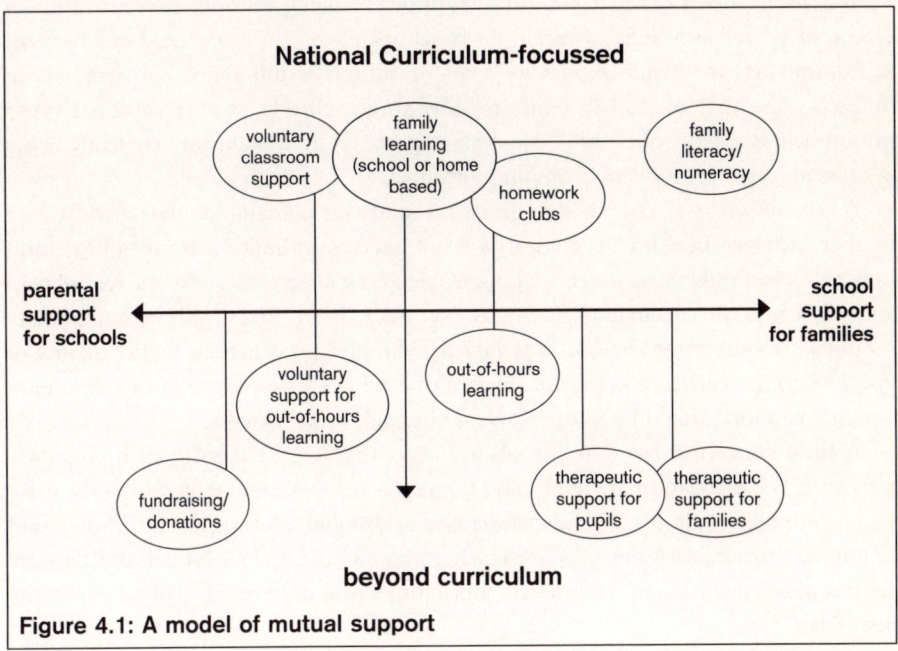

Figure 4.1: A model of mutual support

At the extremes of this axis lie broad motivations: at one end, parental volunteerism that clearly benefits the school more than any individual child. At the other, 'wrap-around' support services for families that have far deeper objectives than the raising of a pupil's achievement. Yet clearly, all of the activities can be mutually beneficial.

This chapter scopes issues relating to the school-based forms of support outlined above. A central premise of this chapter is *that all of the activities it describes should remain voluntary*. Parents cannot be pressganged into public participation in children's learning and the wider social agenda is not one that can be forced on schools. Both, however, can clearly be facilitated and incentivised. Attitudes can be changed, but any increase in rights and duties should be self-generated. Again, the issues of school culture and teacher training rear their heads.

Parental Support for Schools

By far the most common way for parents to support their child's school is through private support of their own child's learning, as described in the preceding and following chapters. Yet many parents go far beyond this involvement to forms of public and civic engagement with their children's schools.

Should voluntary support be encouraged?

Variations in levels of such voluntary support between schools are enormous, a symptom as well as a cause of variations in school effectiveness. Parental involvement in fundraising, for instance, can be a major source of difference between school budgets, one that obviously tends to advantage schools in more affluent areas (Mountfield & Eastwood, 2000). This is an equity question that is not currently being addressed by national or local funding formulae.

A second worry is expressed in an NFER study on parental involvement: 'it may be that such practical involvement in a school serves to limit access to information from schools if only those parents who are able and willing to 'service' the school gain an insight into the curriculum' (Jowett & Baginsky, 1991: 201). Although nationally produced resources for *The Learning Journey* will give parents a far higher quality of insight into the curriculum, part of the aim of a school's strategy to attract voluntary parental support should be to open access channels to *all* parents.

A third concern exists that schools are becoming over reliant on such voluntary activities. The mechanics of literacy and numeracy lessons, especially during the early years, is in many schools fairly dependent on additional adult support, through paid or unpaid learning assistants. As one teacher wrote in the ATL/IPPR survey, 'Bankers are not assisted by unpaid volunteers; they employ the right number of people in the first place'.

Yet schools are not banks, and have social goals that are assisted by voluntary relationships with members of the community they serve. Voluntary parental support should be encouraged in all schools, with three conditions attached:

1. *Schools should have the right to refuse the voluntary support of any individuals or organisations.*
2. *Parents who choose not to volunteer should not have second class access to any school resources, human or physical.*
3. *Nationally imposed initiatives and structures should not require or assume voluntary support.*

Forms of involvement

Fundraising and donations
In most schools, a range of creative initiatives is now complementing more traditional activities such as jumble sales. Also, individual parents are being used as voluntary 'professional fundraisers' as schools make a delayed but enthusiastic entry into the bidding culture. More worrying are the requests for 'voluntary donations', often from schools with an existing air of exclusivity.

Classroom support and participation in out-of-hours learning
Although statistical evidence does not exist, labour market shifts, particularly the huge increase in working mothers, do not appear to have reduced the time and enthusiasm for such parental support (Wragg et al, 1998). Certainly, schools which actively seek parental volunteers, and train them appropriately, build up a considerable resource, and one that gives far greater benefits than can be measured by the mere number of volunteer hours. Such voluntary support, especially when attached to training and accreditation, is often a pathway to learning or paid employment as a learning support assistant. Parental support for out of hours clubs, often unconnected to formal learning, often serves as a first step for less confident parents in engaging with a school and supporting their children's academic learning.

School-based family learning
Family learning has a broad definition, one explored in detail in the Campaign for Learning's new manifesto (Campaign for Learning et al, 2000). This section concentrates on formal, explicit family learning that is carried out in a school setting. In this case, parents are volunteering in schools, but in a way that supports their own learning as well as their child's. Family literacy and numeracy programmes, for instance, aim to assist parents and children simultaneously with their basic skills, giving parents the skills and strategies to help their children both at home and at school. Evaluations of family learning projects have shown improvements in pupil and adult achievement, as well as an increase in parental involvement in home learning (NFER, 1997). Many family learning programmes lead to some form of accreditation, and thus create a progression route for parents to re-engage with lifelong learning opportunities (McCormick, 1999). Many parents also move from family learning activities into volunteering at their child's school.

For social policymakers, therefore, the possibilities of family learning are seductive; the concept has built up an impressive range of support from current provision through the DfEE's Standards Fund, to the Home Office document Supporting Families, to the recent Schools' Plus Report from the Social Exclusion Unit. The literacy task force and the Moser report on basic skills recommend the extension of family learning opportunities (Moser, 1999).

In truth, as last year's IPPR/Scottish Council Foundation study concludes, 'not enough is known about the effectiveness of different local methods of producing gains in attainment and participation that last beyond the initial evaluation period' (McCormick, 1999: 24). Robson and Dyson's review of family learning evaluations point to some 'complexities' in the literature, particularly the diversity of methodologies, and a neglect in exploring the processes that could explain why some parents participate and some do not (Robson & Dyson, 1999). The DfEE's Standards Fund programmes for family literacy and numeracy are already adding coherence and clarity to a previously patchy field.

To perceive family learning as a magic bullet to solve social and educational ills could damage its efficacy. Some of the goals that family programmes intend to meet require additional interventions, such as those described in the section below on 'therapeutic support'. Large scale, longitudinal research is undoubtedly needed, although the objectives of programmes should never be reduced to number crunching on exam performance or adult participation in formal learning. As the IPPR/SCF study argued, 'the task is to enhance the value of existing empirical indicators, not replace them'; to make what is currently too woolly into something wearable.

Although targeted intervention is necessary, another issue concerns the possibility that family learning could become over-targeted towards remedial activities in areas of social exclusion. This could lead to stigmatisation and an unnecessarily limited range of programmes. West Walton Primary School in Norfolk is an excellent example of a school that takes family learning beyond the three Rs. Cheshire LEA's Family Education Programme has developed a 'Families Learning Together' programme in collaboration with their FE partners. Mainly targeted in areas of significant economic disadvantage, the programme uses modules ranging from creative arts to learning through leisure.

Issues and opportunities

Although it is generally assumed that affluent parents are more likely to become involved as active volunteers, the exceptions are numerous. There are hundreds of examples of schools in vastly different catchment areas succeeding in building up significant numbers of parent volunteers. The reasons for this difference go far deeper than their volunteering mechanisms, into the atmosphere and culture of individual schools. Barriers and incentives to participation exist that need to be considered at national and school levels if inclusive volunteering is to be encouraged. Literature concerning parents as volunteers is rare; research on the motivations of parents who do and do not volunteer would be especially useful. The following issues therefore all require further research evidence:

Building school-based volunteering into a civic culture

The government is attempting to create an inclusive 'volunteering culture', as is perceived to exist in North America, through several initiatives. Yet unless these initiatives specifically target schools, or schools tap into such programmes, pupils may be excluded from the benefits. For example, the *Lifelong Learning* paper includes suggestions for adults to be trained by voluntary organisations whilst volunteering. They recommend playgroups and community centres, but not schools. Schools should not be denied this opportunity purely because they do not have charitable status. The Millennium Volunteers programme has also recognised the need to direct more of its volunteers to schools.

The following possibilities are all untested:

- *An exam syllabus or a citizenship curriculum could be designed to stimulate the involvement of parents and secondary pupils in primary schools.*

    For instance, a GCSE/GNVQ Maths or English module could be designed whereby students work as a volunteer for a primary school's literacy or numeracy lesson, planning group work and writing evaluations. This may involve parents returning to learning, or secondary pupils who can provide vital role models for their younger siblings' attitudes to learning.

- *Schools could create their own Local Exchange Trading Schemes (LETS).*

    LETS exist throughout the country, enabling individuals to swap skills using an alternative community currency. Amazingly, none are currently based on schools. Such a scheme, run by one or several schools, could stimulate parents to use their existing skills to support the school in practical and intellectual ways, as well as being an important conduit in the forging of school-based social capital.

- *Schools could train and employ New Deal clients.*

    This could be especially useful for young parents and especially fathers, many of whom are in the New Deal for 18-24 year olds or New Deal for lone parents client groups. Unemployed parents could be trained to work either on school premises, doing building maintenance, for instance, or in classrooms as learning support assistants. As a consequence, this could begin to break down barriers between these parents and their child's school and learning.[1]

Avoiding exclusivity

There are many stories about schools with an active core of parents who effectively form 'volunteer cliques'; an inner circle with easy access to teachers, school information and gossip. Their intimate knowledge of school processes and personnel can intimidate and put off other would-be volunteers. These divisions often have class or racial undercurrents. Parent volunteering can therefore serve to make a school more unwelcoming to the parents who already feel remote from the school. This situation can only be pre-empted by sensitive management from the headteacher or teacher responsible for voluntary support.

Time

Along with childcare difficulties, time is frequently cited as a factor militating against all involvement in volunteering. School-based volunteering could certainly offer more flexible opportunities, and the increase in out of hours learning could facilitate this. Yet there could also be options for parental leave legislation to be more creatively structured to facilitate adult involvement in their children's education, both at home and at school. Recent legislation rigidly locates new leave rights in a child's first five years (eighteen years in the case of parents with disabled children). Parents may need time during a child's school career to contribute to their child's learning or school.

Future parental leave legislation should consider the option of extending 'emergency' family leave to wider activities such as supporting their child's school. Some of this leave should be ringfenced for fathers, whether resident, stepfather or other, on a 'use it or lose it' basis.

Employers should not need to wait for legislation to initiate this. Why should companies release employees for jury service and the Territorial Army, but not for involvement in their children's schools?

Box 4.1

Project Appleseed, an American not-for-profit educational charity, promotes volunteering through the Parental Involvement Pledge. The pledge states that the parent will volunteer a minimum of five hours each semester in activities such as tutoring, serving as a teacher's aide, or supervising extracurricular activities. The pledge is based on the notion that parents are the owners of the state school system and therefore bear a responsibility to participate in the system as ultimate accountability rests with them. Project Appleseed also suggests that employers give every employee ten paid hours of volunteer time per annum in the nation's schools.

Management and training issues

This has two strands: one, if parent volunteers are inadequately prepared for the tasks they are asked to perform, they soon become burdensome on teachers' time ('another person to look after' as one teacher said), or gain nothing from volunteering.

There are plenty of examples of good practice. For instance, at the Chatsworth Computer Project in Liverpool more than 900 parents have been trained in computer skills to help primary teachers. At the London Language and Literacy Unit courses are run in parental involvement in education, including a 'Parents as volunteers' module. Some of the Education Action Zones, for instance Blackburn with Darwen, are also running accredited 'parents as educators' courses. The LLLU also runs a *Peachers* course, which trains parents to teach other parents. Yet this is an area where schools need to develop their own unique practices, to respond to their needs and the make up of their volunteering base.[2]

Two, the management of learning volunteers needs to be built into teacher training and Continuing Professional Development. This is especially relevant if the current Government vision of teachers as 'learning managers' is to be realised.

Consultation

The objectives of voluntary support should be shaped by the combined priorities of the school and the volunteers themselves, yet this is rare. More common is for schools to co-opt volunteers on their terms. The recent evaluation of learning elements of single regeneration budget (SRB) schemes argues that 'the most successful initiatives were those in which the design was based on the views both of the proposed deliverer and the target audience. Unfortunately, the latter group was often ignored' (DfEE, 1999b: 22).

As always, there are exceptions, for instance REACHOut to Parents in Liverpool, which involves parents in the construction of a family learning curriculum. *Any funding bids for the activities described above should require evidence of prior and intended consultation.*

Building in diversity

There is a concern that the government's agenda to raise standards in numeracy and literacy, particularly in primary schools, is pigeonholing volunteering opportunities into these areas. This may put off many possible volunteers through lack of confidence or interest. Schools need to see volunteering as a way of encouraging parents to inspire children or support a school using their particular skills and interests. This can increase the diversity of activities as well as the diversity of the volunteers themselves. The pupils at Ambler School in Finsbury Park, for example, made a film with the

---

Box 4.2 Salusbury World – a school-based refugee centre

15 per cent of children at Salusbury Primary School in Queens Park, London come from refugee families The Salusbury World refugee centre was created in 1999 to offer new, formalised forms of support for these families. The centre's aims are:
- To provide emotional, social and educational support for refugee families
- To raise the self–esteem of refugee parents and children
- To integrate refugee parents with the rest of the school

To assist funding, Salusbury World is registered as a charity, and received a secondee from Business in the Community to support fundraising and implementation. Most of the costs have been met by a National Lottery grant.

The centre has also become a locus for parent volunteers who assist in running the project and offer resources. Since the creation of the centre, the parent volunteer programme across the school now includes many refugee parents.
http://www.salusbury.brent.sch.uk

support of two parent producers and directors. Giving parents a voice in the content of a school's curriculum could help to generate diverse forms of voluntary parental support (see chapter 7).

Targeting paternal involvement
It is a generally agreed concern that most parental volunteers are female, perpetuating the gender imbalance in most primary schools and some secondary schools. For instance, it is estimated that more than 90 per cent of participants in family learning are mothers (McCormick, 1999).

This is worth redressing on a number of counts. The importance of paternal interest in a child's education was documented in chapter 1. Fathers may prefer to show this interest through private, out of school activities. However, as well as the (oft-disputed) 'positive role model (for underachieving boys)' arguments, the low participation of fathers as volunteers deprives schools of a wide range of skills and experiences. Involvement in schools could also be a way of encouraging non-resident fathers to participate in their child's learning.

The question of how fathers can be encouraged to participate remains unanswered. Barrier theories abound, from the hostile 'feminisation' of primary schools, to the 'demonisation' of men as potential abusers, to a male fear of looking 'awkward, incompetent or stupid' (Family Action Centre, 1997). Men are less frequent visitors to the school gates at the beginning and end of school and even when unemployed often have patterns of activity which keep them busy in the daytime. Current examples of relatively successful, targeted intervention are rare. *The Fathercare Project* in South West Sydney, Australia, organises an accreditation in fathercare, and holds competitions for schools to build up the most 'fathercare hours' (Family Action Centre, 1997). There are also School-based *Dads and Reading* projects in several LEAs, and similar schemes for imprisoned fathers. Children North East set up *Fathers Plus* in 1997 to encourage fathers' involvement in primary schools. This is being extended to nursery schools as part of a SureStart programme. Bristol's Community Education Service co-ordinates a men's family learning development project, where fathers have been brought into a primary school as mentors and to take part in 'taster courses' in, for instance, computing and bricklaying. Some schools are also initiating 'bring your dad to school' days.

It seems likely that school-based voluntary support from fathers will not increase unless they are specifically targeted. The DfEE's or LEA's Standards Funds could ringfence resources for such targeting. However, the question of whether the institutional cultures of schools are preventing wider voluntary participation by men needs to be addressed. Other groups that should be targeted include grandparents and childminders.

The secondary decline

School-based parental participation undoubtedly declines as pupils move to secondary school. This is partly unavoidable, as pupils become keener to maintain home-school boundaries. Yet the lack of parental volunteers deprives secondary schools of a valuable resource, and many parents might actually prefer to volunteer with older pupils. Because there is little history of such involvement, secondary schools wishing to encourage volunteers need to be more proactive than primary schools. The Basic Skills Agency evaluation of secondary school projects found that although over 90 per cent of schools included an objective of involving parents, 'attempts by schools to involve parents in the programmes were generally on the margins of the work undertaken, and therefore unsuccessful' (Basic Skills Agency, 1998: 3). Canadian research has argued that school restructuring, into smaller units and with pupils retaining the same form tutor for more than a year, could increase parental volunteering (McKenna & Williams, 1998).

One opportunity for secondary schools is to focus involvement before or at the crucial point of transition. Rush Common Junior School and Fitzharry's Secondary School in Oxfordshire hold joint parent and pupil curriculum workshops with Year 6 and 7 pupils and parents.

Box 4.3 Using parent volunteers to assist transition

↑ Moving On Up ↑ is co-ordinated by Leicester LEA, in partnership with Community Service Volunteers. The project has identified a number of children in eight primary schools who are felt to be at risk from the negative effects of transition to secondary schools. Parents of these and other children are trained to ease transition, working with these children on a one-to-one basis during Year Six and during a child's first year of secondary school. The parent volunteer thus becomes the link for the child between primary and secondary schools.

In the first year of the project, no children who took part in the project were excluded from their secondary school. Many of the parents have increased their involvement with the school.

At **Agnes Stewart CofE High School in Leeds**, the 'Fresh Start' project devised a programme for Year Seven students, with emotional and behavioural difficulties, and their parents. It was recognised that these children had not found the primary-secondary transition easy. Special Needs Assistants and parents take part in 'tracking' pupils from day to day. Parents and children receive accreditation. The programme has not yet been evaluated in terms of academic results or exclusion rates.

There are many examples of projects aimed at the pre-school to primary transition, for instance, **Supporting Parents on Kids' Education** (SPOKES). This research project uses parenting groups and literacy groups to help children settle into their first year of primary school. The project is funded by the Department of Health.

School-based support for families

Schools have a long history of offering advice and support to encourage parents to support their children's learning, either through the school-based activities described above, or through out of school activities described in the following chapter. Although this has always occurred, there has also been a rapid increase in the creation of school-based (although not normally teacher-led) structures that provide more direct forms of family support. The focus very much remains pupil-centred, aiming ultimately to raise achievement, but the activities are more far reaching. Schools are, in a sense, recognising the centrality of factors that may traditionally have been seen as 'peripheral'. This is especially true in areas where families face a higher risk of breakdown or other problems. Family support activities include:

- Counselling programmes for whole families, often those at risk of breakdown.
- Support for families with children at risk of exclusion, truancy, or criminality.
- Parenting programmes.
- Support related to parenting orders.
- Use of home-school link workers (see chapter 8).

Family support is an excellent example of where a variety of services are working in isolation to solve the same problems. The government is keen to promote the idea of collaborative multi-agency support. The school can play a central part in this process, both physically and organisationally. This idea of 'wrap around services' is being trialled in various forms including:

- Education Action Zones, for instance the Family and School Support Team in the Newham EAZ.
- 'full service schools', a term imported from the US, and being piloted in Manchester.
- New Community Schools in Scotland, which give specific focus and resources on the social, emotional and health needs of pupils and their families.

The Social Exclusion Unit's 'Schools Plus' Report has recommended the creation of one-stop Family Support Centres in schools in disadvantaged areas. Schools will be increasingly used as sites for more wide ranging, *therapeutic* support for families in challenging circumstances. The fact that this support is concentrated in areas of social and economic deprivation leaves it open to accusations of creating a 'deficit model', not only of parents, but of a whole community. If schools are to become locations for support services, from counselling to job centres, this should aim in the long term to include as many schools as possible. Developments targeted only at schools in areas of social exclusion could add to the residualisation of such schools. Although focussing on areas of disadvantage is justified and desirable, the long-term vision should be the creation of an unstigmatised school-based family support service, which all parents both can and wish to access.

Changing the purpose of schools so radically can undoubtedly change relationships between parents and schools. Research and practice in the most excluded areas reveal that schools, especially primary schools, are one of the few public service agencies maintaining high levels of social trust (Scottish Council Foundation, 2000). This suggests that primary schools can serve as learning gateways for families who have long since given up on the education system, and support gateways for a range of other services. The key question remains whether the inclusion of other agencies into the school setting will raise the trust in these agencies, or lower trust in the school. Vincent argues that schools' contacts with other agencies can already alienate parents from the school; 'The school appears to form part of a "wall" made up of the "caring professions", backed up by the police and designed to "manage" the local population' (Vincent, 1996: 475). Schools should be used as loci for family support, but not social management or control.

The pace of support for family support initiatives is not matched by the quality of evidence that programmes have delivered impacts on families or pupil achievement (Robson & Dyson, 1999). Yet this and the other issues discussed above should be an incentive for the pilot schemes that are already occurring and being extended. This agenda is being taken forward rapidly, following the recommendations of the Schools Plus Policy Action Team (Social Exclusion Unit, 2000).[3] A final issue, to be discussed in the final chapter, is whether multi-agency support can be truly successful without joint multi-agency training and networking of professionals.

Surrogate support

Much of the school-based support for pupils does not, in fact, seek to involve parents. In reality, breakfast clubs, mentoring schemes and even homework clubs, aim to

---

Box 4.4 CHANCE UK – Mentoring for Parents and Children

Currently working in Islington and Hackney, CHANCE aims to offer early intervention for young children who are at risk of long term behavioural problems. Partly funded by the Home Office, it provides trained mentors for vulnerable primary school children. In addition, it is offering a separate ParentPlus mentoring programme for the parents and carers of children being mentored. This helps ensure that the involvement of an outside agency in their child is an empowering a process as possible.

www.chanceuk.com

some extent to substitute themselves for something that is perceived as a family predicament that is not conducive to learning. This is not a reason to oppose such activities, but these programmes need to aim to nurture rather than deplete the wellsprings of parental engagement with their children's learning. In the Blackburn with Darwen Education Action Zone some of the extra resources for out of hours learning activities have been dedicated to training parents in participating and leading these activities.

Policy conclusions

This chapter has attempted to map a busy but nonetheless patchy field. Although some interesting projects have been identified, the purpose of this report is not to evaluate the quality of competing programmes. All of the areas scoped above should increase in all sectors, but should remain voluntary for both schools and families. More general conclusions that can be drawn are:

At the national and local levels:

- Nationally imposed initiatives should not demand or assume voluntary support.
- Family Learning activities should be diversified and targeted. National and LEA Standards Funds should be altered to:
    - extend family learning beyond literacy and numeracy
    - encourage parental involvement activities that deliberately target fathers, grandparents and childminders
    - grant funding for primary and secondary schools to collaborate in encouraging parental involvement at transition points
- Any funding bids for school-based activities that require voluntary parental support should require evidence of prior and intended parental consultation.
- An exam syllabus or a citizenship curriculum should be designed to stimulate the involvement of parents and secondary pupils in primary schools.
- The management of learning volunteers needs to be built into teacher training and Continuing Professional Development.
- A success criterion for any surrogate support activity should be to increase parental involvement in a child's learning.

At school level:

- Schools should have the right to refuse the voluntary support of any individuals or organisations.
- Parents who choose not to volunteer should not have second class access to any school resources, human or physical.
- Schools should investigate the idea of creating their own Local Exchange Trading Schemes (LETS).[4]
- Schools should explore the opportunity to train and employ New Deal clients.

Further research is required on:

- the motivations of parents who do and do not choose to volunteer
- the long term effectiveness of different family learning models
- out-of-hours learning activities that successfully engage children *and* their parents

A key question remains as to the role of teachers and other school staff in these programmes, and in particular the family support agenda. This question will be addressed in the concluding chapter.

Endnotes

1   This idea is explored in more detail in McCormick J (1999).
2   For a useful toolkit, see National Support Project for Secondary Schools (2000) *How to... Provide training for volunteers and learning support assistants* London: Basic Skills Agency.
3   For a more detailed account of school–based support for families, see Ball M (1998), The Social Exclusion Unit Policy Action Team 11 (2000).
4   IPPR will be initiating this idea in schools from January 2000. Anyone interested in the idea should contact us.

5. Home-based support

However successful and comprehensive the school-based mutual support described in the previous chapter becomes, the bulk of parental involvement in a child's learning is likely to remain home-based. The term 'home-based' encompasses both learning activities carried out around the home, and out of school learning activities where parental involvement ranges from merely paying fees to running an organisation.

The widening role of learning beyond the classroom is documented elsewhere (Bentley, 1998). What needs further consideration is the way in which these forms of learning impact on family-school relationships. The dimensions of home-based learning can enhance and damage these relationships, asking searching questions about ownership and control of children's learning. A key question is how the promotion of home-based learning can assist those who are most in need of such additional study time and support, rather than further benefit the already advantaged.

The home as a learning institution

The home environment has long been recognised as offering a distinct, alternative learning environment, from the pre-school years, when around 80 per cent of all language development takes place, through to post-compulsory education. Hannon sets out the contrasting qualities of home and school below (Hannon, 1993). Although his description of the school setting is too damning and of the home setting too idealistic, the comparison is nonetheless useful:

Box 5.1 Learning at school and at home	
School	*Home*
• shaped by curriculum • bounded by sanctions • timetabled • contrived problems • restricted language • limited conversations • special resources – limited access • recognition of achievement in approved area • horizontal age group • distant relationship with adults • pupil role • accounts for little variation in academic achievement	• shaped by interest • spontaneous • flexible • natural problems • everyday language • extended conversations • 'natural' resources – unlimited access • recognition of achievement in many areas • vertical age group • close relationship with adults • multiple roles • accounts for much variation in academic achievement

A central fear is that, if home learning becomes over-institutionalised or colonised as the evening and weekend outpost of schooling, this may dilute its unique qualities. The aim must be to mould the fabric of home learning to ensure that it retains its richness and diversity; home-based learning should aim to be family-like, not school-like. Schools undoubtedly recognise home learning as a possibly irreplaceable factor in pupil achievement. Yet current policy towards home-based learning may be increasing the expected quantity whilst reducing the breadth.

At the same time, tensions may arise when the pedagogies of home and school clash; in many conflicts, it is parents not schools who are the 'forces of conservatism'. The Holy Grail is consistency without uniformity, but as a compromise, neither may be better than both.

School-initiated home-based learning

Many schools do encourage spontaneous, informal parental engagement with their children's learning. However, the most crucial method that schools use is coercive, through homework, rather than optional.

Homework

Homework does not only spoil weekends; it can turn homes into semi-permanent war zones. It could be argued that homework is a necessary evil, one that a combination of efficient schooling and extended hours for independent learning at school could render unnecessary.

However, homework has the corresponding power to improve relationships between parent and child, giving them a focus through which to interact. It is also the key continuous interface between home and school upon which the success of all other home-school links can be built or broken. Homework is one of the few ways in which parents can monitor a teacher's style and performance. Every school's curriculum is designed with the assumption that some work will be carried out at home, and that other family members will be available to assist with elements of this work.

Current policy and practice

There is no reason to dispute Ofsted's conclusion that 'when [homework is] used properly, it extends the challenge open to the pupil and ensures that teaching time is used to maximum effect.' (1996-7 Ofsted Annual Report in DfEE, 1998c: 3). The revitalisation of homework procedures can also be a key factor in school improvement (Social Exclusion Unit, 2000).

There is also consensus, supported by the findings of Ofsted and NFER, that its improper use is widespread. Government policy has aimed to improve the quantity and quality of homework. As well as giving recommended times for different age groups, the DfEE's homework guidance advises that homework policies must be drawn up in consultation with parents, and that home-school agreements need to contain information about homework (DfEE, 1998c).

Although evidence has yet to emerge, it seems clear that, especially at primary level, pupils are now being set more homework than ever. This is probably more as a result of statutory legislation, such as national tests, associated targets, and an increase in GCSE coursework than the guidance above.

Families' views of homework
Recent surveys have found that parents are generally satisfied with the amounts of homework that children are now receiving.[2] Concerns focus on the nature of homework, and the parental role. Parents are often critical of a school's failure to communicate its homework policies effectively or provide sufficient explanation of the purposes and goals of particular pieces of homework. Homework is also often seen as poorly set, and marked late. In addition, parents report that teachers do not always seem to be aware of how long it takes pupils to do particular pieces of homework (Cowan & Hallam, 1999). There is also a widespread confusion about expectations, and lack of confidence about the tasks set, particularly in mathematics (DfEE and MORI survey, 1999).[3]

Pupils have similar sentiments, with particular concerns about marking. In a BBC poll, 60 per cent of pupils wanted increased input from their parents. Yet there is also evidence that children deliberately avoid parental input, or manipulate their parents by feigning difficulties and persuading the parent to complete homework on their behalf (Edwards *et al*, 2000).

Clearly, good homework practice is common, where parents do understand and enjoy their role as homework facilitators. Yet there is an underlying set of issues that need to be thought through at all levels.

What is the parental role in homework?
If there is general confusion about the parental role, this may be because two of the central purposes of homework are partly contradictory. These are:

- To encourage independence, organisation and self-discipline
- To encourage parents to support their child's learning, offering one to one support that is rarely available in the classroom

Homework policies can offer some transparency, yet in any school, different pieces of homework are likely to require differential input. Both parental under and over-involvement can be detrimental to pupil achievement. Schools need to be explicit about the expected role of parents in any piece of homework. Homework diaries are useful communication tools. Communication about homework is especially important at the primary/secondary transition stage, when parents are particularly confused about their more limited role. *Research is, however, urgently needed to establish what kind of parental support is most productive under what circumstances.*

What kinds of home learning should schools promote?

On the one hand, if homework mainly consists of closed activities, relying for instance on worksheets (or, ever-frequently, past SATs papers), then schools are denying parents opportunities to tap into the unique attributes of home learning. On the other, more open homework activities, such as research or home experiments, often presume a level of parental skills or family resources that may not exist, or else demand an excessive amount of parental time.

The policy of many schools is that homework should aim to reinforce knowledge and skills learnt in the classroom. Yet within this boundary, opportunities can be harnessed for creative use of all home environments. One example is the Teachers Involve Parents in Schoolwork (TIPS) programme in the US, which promotes homework that requires students to interview family members, elicit parents' experiences, and involve them in real life situations.[4] There are also programmes such as the IMPACT project for maths homework, that specifically aim to involve parents as participants in learning, rather than as supplementary teachers. At the national level, *The Learning Journey* will give parents guidance on home learning activities that are distinct from homework.

Milgram's analysis on homework and individual learning styles is also important. He argues that teachers and counsellors should encourage parents 'to develop an understanding of their children's homework style and to provide conditions for learning at home that match it.' (Milgram & Hong, 1996: 251).[5] As thinking about individual learning styles begins to filter through to schools, parents should not be excluded from its potential benefits. The homework workshops described on the following page are ideal vehicles to communicate this knowledge.

Will home learning widen inequalities?

The answer is, almost inevitably 'yes'. If homework did not exist, most families would generate their own alternative, leaving those children whose parents did not at a disadvantage. By turning the optional into the compulsory, homework can transform home learning from a random privilege into a universal right.

However, recent political and social developments may have created a paradox; as governments' and schools' expectations of what parents should contribute to a child's educational development at home have risen, social and economic developments have simultaneously rendered such contributions more difficult for many families. Homework can also exacerbate the intergenerational effect of poor basic skills (Moser, 1999).

In addition, homework may widen inequalities through promoting a certain set of 'learning norms', and therefore denying other styles, forming yet another piece in the 'deficit' jigsaw. Many supportive strategies aim to prevent homework from being a factor that widens inequalities in achievement. Although they are worthy of discussion, they also appear as damage limitation exercises, rather than solutions. Unless the still-widening inequalities between family resources and motivations are reversed, this may be all we can expect from them.

School support for parents with home learning

Universal support

The most common form of universal support is through open meetings that either transmit information or allow parents to share information about a particular curriculum area or learning concern. This is often supported at supra-school level. For instance, the Parents' Information Network organises 'Family web' Internet workshops. These enable school staff to provide structured training and support to parents. This practice is slowly spreading to Secondary Schools, and also to the key point of primary to secondary transition. Manchester LEA, for instance, has initiated a project to involve parents of Year 7 children in their homework called PATCH (parents and their children's homework).

Box 5.2

Whitley Bay High School has pioneered a series of workshops to raise parents' confidence in supporting their children's learning, with handouts available for those unable to attend. After consultation with parents, sessions were planned that focussed on general issues rather than the subject-based sessions. Subjects included:

- helping your child to learn
- talking with your teenager
- talking about drugs
- window on technology

www.whitleybayhighschool.org

Schools are also using other mechanisms to raise parents' confidence levels. Wrockwardine Infants School in Telford, and the 'Parents Count' organisation in London produce videos with parents to share home learning ideas (www.parentscount.roundel.net). New innovations also include 'homework hotline' answerphone services for parents, and an e-mail homework support service accompanied by an on-line teacher providing assistance at certain hours every evening. In the North East Lincolnshire EAZ, lessons are being videotaped and broadcast during the early evening on a local cable channel to assist children and parents with homework. School support is also being backed up at national level, with new online and paper-based resources.

Targeted support

Much of the targeted support occurs through the mechanisms described in the previous chapter. All family learning and parenting education projects build a home learning element into their programmes. This ranges from advice on learning environments to planning practical activities.

Box 5.3 SHARE

The Community Education Development Centre's (CEDC) SHARE project is now nationally established and used in over thirty LEAs and in over 350 schools. Supported by a trained worker, parents create and work through homework materials with their child. 'It works by helping you understand how your child learns, what your child is learning at school and how to work together using learning activities at home.' (Junior Share Book 1, p2). This can lead to accreditation by the Open College Network. Originally practised with the parents of primary school children, SHARE is now extending its activities to offer the following targeted support:

- *Parents as co-educators*, using ICT to encourage parental involvement with secondary school pupils' learning.
- *It's a man thing* grew out of the realisation that few men were participating in SHARE projects, and that none of the fathers who had participated were continuing with the programme.
- *A fair chance* – supporting carers with home-based learning. Currently being piloted in eight LEAs, each local area organises group work sessions for foster carers, targeted at the specific needs to this group. Each area has its own steering group that includes a foster carer, young person, and social services representative.

A SHARE project has also been set up by Leicester LEA in a woman's refuge.

www.cedc.org.uk

Another form of targeting aims to ensure that families do not suffer from the digital divide. In a school in Texas, where 94 per cent of families are below the poverty line, all pupils have been given laptops to assist homework. The laptops become unusable if they are not connected to the school network regularly. The Wednesbury Education Action Zone is also experimenting with laptop loans to families.

A group currently under-targeted is fathers. A BBC poll found that 85 per cent of pupils named the mother as the main source of help with homework (BBC, 1999). Small-scale research found that the percentage of fathers who play with their children, or help with homework daily, falls from 86 per cent before the child is five to 17 per cent during the primary school years (Marsiglio, 1991). The Fathers and Reading Scheme, piloted through the National Year of Reading, is one example of targeted encouragement, but others are urgently needed. Under the Family Support Grants programme, a number of voluntary organisations have also been funded to develop work specifically with fathers.

Study support

Study support is, in effect, another form of surrogate support, as described in the previous chapter. Part of its purpose is to act as substitute for what is implicitly viewed as an unsatisfactory home learning environment. Not always school-based, homework clubs and other study support initiatives are receiving enormous amounts of funding through the New Opportunities Fund and other public, private and voluntary organisations. Targeted at areas of disadvantage, sufficient funding is now being provided to support 50 per cent of all secondary and special schools and 25 per cent of all primary schools.

This symptom-attacking strategy will need to be carefully monitored during the next decade. Although the DfEE's Code of Practice on study support advises that parents are involved, there is a risk that such initiatives may further entrench the non-participation of some families in their children's learning. In particular, evidence is needed of study support initiatives that raise both pupil achievement and parental involvement levels. This does not mean that parents need to attend homework clubs; but these clubs should as far as possible aim to raise the motivation for parents to increase levels of home-based support. The Social Exclusion Unit Policy Action Team 11's report recommends the introduction of neighbourhood learning centres, where pupils and parents can learn skills alongside each other (Social Exclusion Unit, 2000).

Parent-initiated home-based learning

Parents have always educated their children, formally and informally, in and around the home. By comparison, the century and a half of mass schooling is a drop in the educational ocean. In spite of time pressures, more parents than ever seem to be using the growing range of resources, methods and technologies to contribute to their child's out of school learning. The scope of this report is not to map these developments, but to examine how such home learning influences home-school relationships.

Learning, or schooling?

One possible tension, already described, is that the increased amounts of homework described above may limit opportunities for alternative forms of parental input. Yet the enormous growth in sales of 'national curriculum-related/Pass Your SATs' workbooks, designed for children aged three and upwards, shows that parents are limiting these opportunities themselves. Why is this occurring? Part of the reason must be the ease of 'off the shelf' learning activities. Yet it also shows the extent to which parents have bought into the national tests culture, confining home learning to yet more coaching for tests. This development is worrying. Such learning may not actually be better than nothing. *Both educational publishers and the government need to take responsibility to ensure that home learning activities are wide in range, and do not merely replicate schooling.*

Use of other educators

The traditional parental involvement in, and encouragement of, extra-curricular activities, both school and non-school, have generally dovetailed happily with school hours learning. Such activities are becoming available to the vast majority through the massive increase in out of hours learning described in the previous chapter. A trend that may have more impact on family-school relationships is the increased parental use of other educators to increase their child's formal, curriculum-based learning. The two main sources are:

- individual or group private tuition, the use of which is growing in the UK, US and Asia
- additional schooling from voluntary supplementary schools, often with religious or cultural objectives

The driver for this demand is a parental concern that mainstream schools are not meeting a child's academic and, additionally in the latter case, cultural needs. Yet this demand has its own momentum, fuelled by rising disposable incomes, that school improvement could never repel. Nor should it wish to. These are valid and valuable statements of parental interest in their child's education that schools should build links with, again aiming for consistency without uniformity. Schools can also learn from how these market-based organisations communicate with parents and satisfy their demands. The case of supplementary schools is discussed in appendix 3.

New technologies

The growth in online learning possibilities and the forthcoming explosion of digital learning channels provide parents with an ever-expanding range of resources through which to educate their child. ICT developments are already helping to undermine the hegemony of the school as font of knowledge and teacher as font of knowledge communication. But for schools and families, the opportunity to network home and school learning has incredible potential. In most cases, home learning will dovetail with and supplement learning that takes place at school. Yet significant challenges may be posed from families who interpret such forms of learning as superior to what the school can offer.

To pick three examples from hundreds:

- *Digitalbrain* from educentre.com offers comprehensive online educational content through subject PowerStations. The content covers the whole National Curriculum. The PowerStations provide tutored guides to each course, with attainment targets, exercises and reviewed hyperlinks to the web sites for every subject. They also provide a structured format for storing work online. Two way e-mail communication is possible.

- *Anytime Anywhere Learning* (AAL) sponsored mainly by Microsoft and Compaq, is now being implemented in the UK. It is designed to give students 24-hour access to laptops and information online. Initial findings relating to the project in the UK point to the significant benefits for individual pupils, but warn that parents are likely to have high expectations of the project and that 'the form and frequency of communication between homes and schools should be negotiated at the outset.' (TES, 16.4.99).

- *Notschool.net* from Ultralab (a research centre supported by Anglia Polytechnic University) offers an alternative form of learning, tailored for pupils who, for various reasons ranging from long-term ill health to truancy to exclusion, are not attending school. It creates an on-line virtual community of teenagers, placed out of school for the reasons noted above, with local clusters supported both electronically, and in some cases face to face, by teacher facilitators at a ratio of one to four. Among the programme's objectives for students are:
    - to raise their self esteem as learners to encourage a return to learning through seduction, not coercion
    - to pass some examinations – evidence accredited learning
    - to build their capabilities as potential net contributors to the UK economy
    - to enhance their ICT capability

The explosion of ICT home learning packages is undoubtedly creating confusion and nervousness amongst families about how ICT changes their role as homework facilitators, and about the quality of products that their children are using. It is interesting that educational CD-ROMs, many of dubious quality, have been far more popular with families than with schools. There is no doubt that parents need guidance over the ever-expanding choices of hardware and educational software.

Schools may not have the time or expertise to offer such support, but a national quality control system may lead to a rigid kitemarking system. One option is described below.

> **Box 5.4 The PIN Educational Software Evaluation Scheme for Parents**
>
> The Parents Information Network established an educational software evaluation scheme for parents in 1996. It receives funding support and endorsement from the DfEE.
> This scheme involves a national evaluator network of 107 teachers and parents who evaluate software for use in the home environment by parents and their children. There is a dedicated full-time Scheme Manager who co-ordinates and trains all evaluators, providing special support to parent evaluators. 70 UK software publishers already submit products to the PIN scheme. Programs meeting the standards of published PIN criteria are awarded the PIN Quality Marks in either Approved or Gold categories. These Marks were established in 1996 and are used by over 70 per cent of submitting publishers.
>
> www.pin.org.uk

In terms of new technology, schools are faced with two distinct and growing challenges. First, until schools can offer one computer per child, their technology resources will always lag behind those of many families. Such families may begin to see home-based online learning as superior to what the school can offer. But if students are engaged in individualised home learning packages, schools have an opportunity to refocus their objectives, and essentially play to their strengths. This could involve, for instance, an increase in collaborative learning or the creative application of knowledge.

Second, and more crucially, schools, with the support of libraries and alternative learning centres, have a key role to play in offering digital learning opportunities to families without access to such resources. The government's commitment to access to the internet for all by 2005, depends on schools taking on this role. The ICT-driven 'community learning centre' concept is a huge opportunity to bring parents into a school setting, but to re-engage with learning (both with and without their children) on their own terms.

The vast majority of schools will need to cater for both the situations expressed above. Schools are in the awkward but potentially powerful position of straddling the digital divide. IPPR's current digital media and education project, @school, will investigate ICT and home-school relationships in more detail.

Home schooling

As the ultimate form of parental involvement, home schooling deserves attention; those who practice it are enthusiastic and vocal, yet it has little impact on the mainstream education system.

Section 7 of the 1996 Education Act places a duty on the DfEE and LEAs to have regard to the general principle that pupils are to be educated in accordance with their parents' wishes, including home schooling. LEAs have a duty to ensure that home education is suitable, although there is no obligation to follow the national curriculum.

Estimates on the numbers of children being educated at home range from 7,000 to over 25,000, or 0.5 per cent of all school aged children.[6] Numbers are approximate because LEAs are informed when children have been removed from their schools, but not where they are being educated.

In the US, approximately 350,000 are home educated, and evidence is coming from many Western nations that numbers are rising. Much of the motivation is dissatisfaction with the school system, but the causes of this dissatisfaction are too varied, and the numbers of children too small, to demand change from the school system. However diverse mainstream schooling becomes, it seems unlikely that these numbers will decline.

Mainstream educators should engage positively with home schoolers, for the simple reason that schools have much to learn from the teaching and learning practices of home educators. As home schooling embraces new technologies, this may become increasingly pertinent.

Flexi-schooling

The idea of flexi-schooling is that parents may wish their children to be educated by the state on a part-time basis, spending other time learning at home, in workplaces or through private provision. Currently, schools are not obliged to let a family pursue this course of education for their child, though it is legal for them to do so. Although there is not at present a significant amount of parents who wish to use the flexi-approach to education, more flexible curricular and working patterns could make this a possibility for many more parents in forthcoming decades. David Hargreaves has predicted that:

> The move away from traditional schooling will be encouraged by business and industry, which will replace conventional company perks such as cars with a range of educational benefits that will make it easier for employees to tutor children at home (Hargreaves, 1997).

This may seem far-fetched, but is in fact already happening. For instance:

- The Portage scheme integrates home teaching by parents with part-time attendance at school.
- Inclusion strategies often aim for the part-time reintegration of excluded pupils or persistent truants.

- Part of the remit of specialist schools is to admit pupils for certain subjects, as is the case with the new links being forged between maintained and independent schools.

- Many parents who were born outside of the UK are sending their children to their country of origin for several months as a key part of their cultural education.

These examples are not rejections of the state system, but recognition of its limitations and resource constraints. Schools therefore should not see flexi-schooling as a threat, but as an impetus to become more flexible themselves and to accommodate individual patterns of learning. If they cannot meet this challenge, then the private sector may become an attractive part-time option for many parents.

Policy conclusions

In many ways, home-based learning is moving in a positive direction. Parents are increasingly willing to be involved.[7] ICT developments are creating exciting new opportunities for such involvement. Family learning projects are supporting parents to engage with their children's learning at home; and an enormous amount of resources is being given to fund alternatives for pupils with limited access to home learning resources or parental support.

Some issues remain. Teachers are acutely aware of the effects of overload, yet many may be in danger of overloading families in a similar fashion, adding to family stress or denying space for parent-initiated learning activities. How can this be avoided? The most important way is for schools to ensure that their communication and participatory structures permit consultation on the amounts of homework. Many schools achieved this as part of their consultations on home school agreements. Another could be for schools' home learning policies to include guidelines that encourage parents to engage in home learning that is totally unconnected with homework.

The other issues that this chapter discussed require consideration at *national, local and school levels*:

- Both educational publishers and the government need to take responsibility to ensure that home learning activities are wide in range and do not merely replicate schooling.

- Homework clubs and other forms of study support should as far as possible aim to raise the motivation for parents to increase levels of home-based support.

- In the long term, schools need to find ways to develop links with home schooled pupils, and actively encourage flexi-schooling as part of individualised learning

- The DfEE should fund (but not run) an intermediary to review and explain digital home learning opportunities for parents.

- The school system should begin to open up to the idea of flexi-schooling. This might include part-time pupils, or pupils who take a one-term sabbatical from school. In this time, pupils could be learning from home, a workplace, or engaged in 'active citizenship'.

Further research is required on:

- What kind of parental support for homework is most productive under what circumstances. This is an ideal opportunity for teacher and parent-led research.

- How the use of ICT resources at home and school might impact on home-school relations.

Endnotes

1. Weston P and Ofsted (1999) *Homework: Learning from practice* London: The Stationary Office. Ofsted claimed that only a quarter of primary schools make good use of homework, and a general lack of coherence in most secondary schools' homework strategies.
2. DfEE and MORI (1999) *Parents and Schools* London: DfEE. In the survey of 1,000 parents of 5-11 year olds, attending primary school, 69 per cent felt their child had the 'right amount' of homework, 18 per cent felt their child had 'too little' homework, and 11 per cent felt their child had 'too much'.
3. A little over half of the parents interviewed always feel confident to help their child do their homework, whilst a third worried that they may be doing it wrong. When it came to helping with maths homework, 14 per cent found it 'difficult'.
4. Teachers Involve Parents in Schoolwork (TIPS) at the Center on School, Family, and Community Partnerships, John Hopkins University. Further information on the TIPS process can be accessed at www.csos.jhu.edu/p2000/tips.htm
5. Analyses of parental involvement in their children's homework is made in relation to children's individual learning style, using the 22 scores on the Learning Style Inventory (Dunn, Dunn, and Price 1984). The argument is put forward that teachers and counsellors should encourage parents 'to develop an understanding of their children's homework style and to provide conditions for learning at home that match it.'

6   In 1996, the DfEE knew of 7,000 children who are not being taught in schools, while Dr Ronald Meighan put the figure at 10,000 (*The Times* 26.4.96 p39). Alexander T (1997) *Family Learning: the foundation of effective learning* London: Demos, puts the estimate at 25,000 (0.5 per cent of all school aged children), but does not substantiate this.

7   70 per cent of parents read daily with their primary aged children (DfEE, 4.8.99).The survey, conducted by the Cabinet Office also showed that the figure rose to four out of five parents or 80 per cent of those with children under five years old.

III: Exit and Voice

6. Parental choice of schools

My fundamental belief is that parental choice will improve standards. And what makes it so powerful is that there will always be the incentive for schools to respond to parental wishes. Parents want the best for their children. We are giving them the chance to seek this...
John Patten, then Secretary of State for Education, 1992 (in David, 1995: 274).

The issue of parental choice generates far more media attention than it deserves, particularly from London-based columnists perpetuating the myth of an exodus to private education. Most children still attend their local school, and do this without having deliberately moved catchment areas. There are many parts of the country where choice is simply not an issue for families.

However, the UK is a genuine 'social laboratory' in the sense that choice and competition have been given such status and priority. Although the right to choose schools is enshrined in the legislation of virtually all EU countries, choice is less of an issue in the rest of Europe. Two decades since parents were given the right to express a preference for one school over another, the intended and unintended outcomes of choice policies and rhetoric are worthy of examination. As well as the impact such policies have on family-school relationships, choice has wider implications for families' and schools' attitudes to their locality.

Choice: objectives and objections

It is virtually taken for granted that, where possible, parents should be able to choose the school that their child attends. Behind this assumption lie three theoretical justifications that are worth unpicking:

Parents' rights

This justification is based on the idea that parents should have liberty to decide how and therefore where their children are educated. There are clear questions about how the rights of one parent may impinge on those of another. For instance, if all parents have a right to send their girls to single-sex schools, and choose to exercise it, how might this affect the rights of parents who wish their boys to attend mixed schools? There are also interesting issues behind why the ideal of choice has become sacred in the education sector, but has, as yet, barely impacted on thinking in health policy.

Equity

Choice has always occurred; part of the justification for its extension was that it should be for the many, not the few. It was hoped that encouraging the assertion of preference and increasing the information available to parents about schools would extend a privilege that was already being used by those 'in the know'. One equity problem with choice, however, is that those with the resources to move to a popular catchment area or pay the travel costs to attend a popular non-local school are still favoured. Another is that it benefits only the children of the choosers, further disadvantaging those children whose parents choose the 'wrong' school, or make no choice at all. This can be seen as an example of what has been described as the shift from a meritocracy to 'parentocracy' (Brown, 1990).

Efficiency

This has two strands: one is that the discipline of the market, through the need to attract pupil numbers, will give schools the impetus to improve their performance. The other is that, through exercising choice, parents will be able to determine school behaviour, thus making schools more responsive to the views of consumers. Yet the creation of genuine choice for all children at all times would require every school to have a permanent surplus of places, which is inherently inefficient. The Audit Commission's recent study of school places admitted 'a potential tension between the policy objectives of, on the one hand, maximising economy and efficiency and, on the other, maximising choice' (Audit Commission, 1996: 45).

A further equity and efficiency consideration arises from our knowledge of the 'peer group effect'. Research outlined in chapter one indicates that the nature of a school's intake has a significant impact on individual pupil performance at GCSE; the lower the socio-economic status of a child, the more significant the effect (Feinstein & Symons, 1999). Thus if choice leads to social segregation, its outcome has been inefficient as external costs may outweigh private benefits.

The political use of choice policies and rhetoric is affected as much by one's views of schools as views of parents. The previous government's faith in parental influence stemmed from a view of state schools as inherently inefficient and prone to producer capture. As the brief review of legislation in the chart below shows, choice policies have been retained by the current government, with minor changes. However, the government no longer appears to see parental choice as a key lever in raising standards, implicitly aiming to reduce the importance of choice, through encouraging schools to act collaboratively, and supporting schools who are faced with the negative effects of choice.

Box 6.1 A Legislative History of School Choice

1944 Education Act s.76
'The Minister and LEAs shall have regard to the general principle that, so far as it is compatible with the provision of efficient instruction and training and the avoidance of unreasonable public expenditure, pupils are to be educated in accordance with the wishes of their parents.'

1980 Education Act
Parents were given the right to express a preference of schools.
The Assisted Places Scheme was introduced.

1988 Education Reform Act
Open enrolment and per-capita funding were introduced, effectively putting a price on every pupil's head.
Parents were given the right to ballot for Grant Maintained Status, and to choose Communication and Technology Colleges.
Parents were given right of appeal to an independent appeal committee, set up by the governors of grant maintained and voluntary aided schools and local education authorities.

1989 Greenwich Judgement
This established that LEA-maintained schools may not give priority to children simply because of the fact that they live in the authority's administrative area.

1991 Parents' Charter (updated 1994)
The section titled 'the right to choose' offered no new rights, but reminded parents of their rights above.

1996 Education Act
The nursery voucher system was introduced.
LEAs were required to make arrangements so that parents could express a school preference, and to meet that preference wherever possible.

1997 Rotherham Judgement
Catchment areas were judged a valid admissions criterion, but schools were ordered to consider the choices of parents who have expressed a preference before considering other criteria.

1998 Schools Standards and Framework Act
The nursery voucher scheme was abandoned.
Admissions appeal panels were made independent from LEAs
An independent Schools Adjudicator was appointed to determine disputes between admission authorities over their admission arrangements.
Foundation schools (a new category of schools, introduced partly to replace GM schools) maintained the right to be their own admissions authorities.
All schools were allowed to admit up to 10 per cent of children on the basis of aptitude in certain subjects.
Admission authorities were required to consult each other before determining their admission arrangements.

1999 School Admissions Code of Practice
This stemmed from the promise held in *Excellence in Schools* to find 'fairer ways of offering school places to pupils.' (DfEE, 1997b: 7). One key principle is that 'the arrangements should meet parents' preferences for the schools of their choice to the maximum extent possible.' (DfEE, 12/98: 8).
- LEAs should attempt to spread the burden of children with challenging behaviour.
- Schools admitting pupils outside the normal year of entry may in certain circumstances refuse admission to children with challenging behaviour.
- Admission authorities should not apply oversubscription criteria to the detriment of certain social groups in the community.

Two decades on, the justifications above need to be judged pragmatically, by examining the intended and unintended outcomes of parental preference legislation.

The effects of parental choice

One problem with discussions over parental choice is that many hark back to a non-existent golden age of admissions, when all children walked happily to their local school. This was never the case. Even before 1980, when LEAs had greater discretion over admissions, and parents had fewer means to complain, choice was still a factor that impacted on schools. Arguably, the legislation of the 1980s was less significant than the accompanying new right rhetoric, which actively encouraged the assertion of preference and harnessed broader processes of rising consumer expectations.

Effects on parents

Parental views of choice

Before parental preference was enshrined in legislation, there was little evidence of a widespread parental dissatisfaction with the existing system. This may be partly because, since choice was not openly promoted, those parents who actively sought alternatives to local provision were in the minority, so could normally access these alternatives. Although there may have been a burgeoning public desire for improved quality across all public services, the Conservatives' policies of the 1980s were used more to create a demand for choice, than to respond to one.

To what extent has that demand now been embedded into parents' thinking? Certainly, even parents who feel that 'schools choose parents, not the other way around', are generally supportive of the principle of choice. In a parental evaluation of Conservative education policies, the only initiative that was universally popular was the 'increased emphasis on parental choice of school' (Boulton & Coldron, 1996a: 299). A review of surveys in 1990 argued that 'nine out of ten parents value choice, whether or not they positively exercise it' (MacBeath & Weir, 1991: 31).

Parents' use of choice

Are parents exercising choice in this way? A review of small-scale research has claimed that 75 per cent of pupils still attend their most local school without visiting alternatives (Smedley, 1995). Clearly, strong incentives to do so remain, relating to convenience, networks and child friendships. However, this figure hides the families who move to specific catchment areas to guarantee their choice of school. What we do know is that the average distance from home to school is shown in Table 6.1 (DETR, 1998a: 41).

Table 6.1 Average journeys to school

	Primary	Secondary
1983-85	1.1 miles	2.3 miles
1995-97	1.3 miles	3.1 miles

This rise can only be partially explained by the closure of small schools.

Another way to analyse their use of choice is to explore the levels of dissatisfaction. The Audit Commission's study of school places showed that 10 per cent of parental preferences were not met, and a further nine per cent did not express their genuine first choice, so sure were they that the application would fail (Audit Commission, 1996). Complaints about admissions and subsequent appeals have risen rapidly since their inception, as Figure 6.1 below shows (DfEE, 2000a).[1]
Since 1997, the number of appeals lodged as a percentage of admissions has plateaued in primary schools, but has risen by nearly one third in secondary schools.

What the graph does not show is the amount of local variation. The numbers of appeals vary greatly between different LEAs, as Figures 6.2 and 6.3 demonstrate.

Many researchers have argued that choice legislation has enabled middle class parents to use their competitive advantage, in order to secure a place at their preferred school. Ball *et al*'s project categorised these parents as the *privileged/skilled*, who have the economic, social and cultural capital to decode school systems and play the choice game most effectively, including appealing if necessary (Ball *et al*, 1996; Reay, 1996; David *et al*,

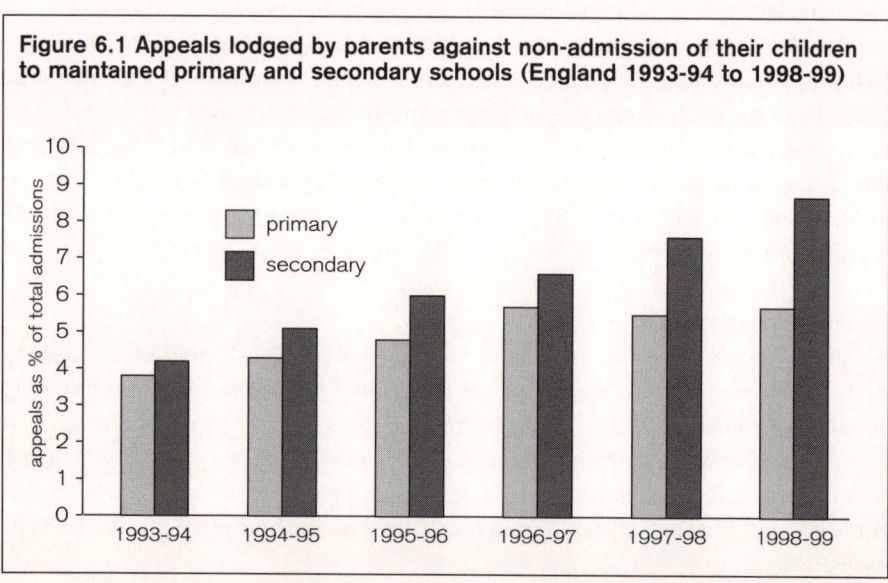

Figure 6.1 Appeals lodged by parents against non-admission of their children to maintained primary and secondary schools (England 1993-94 to 1998-99)

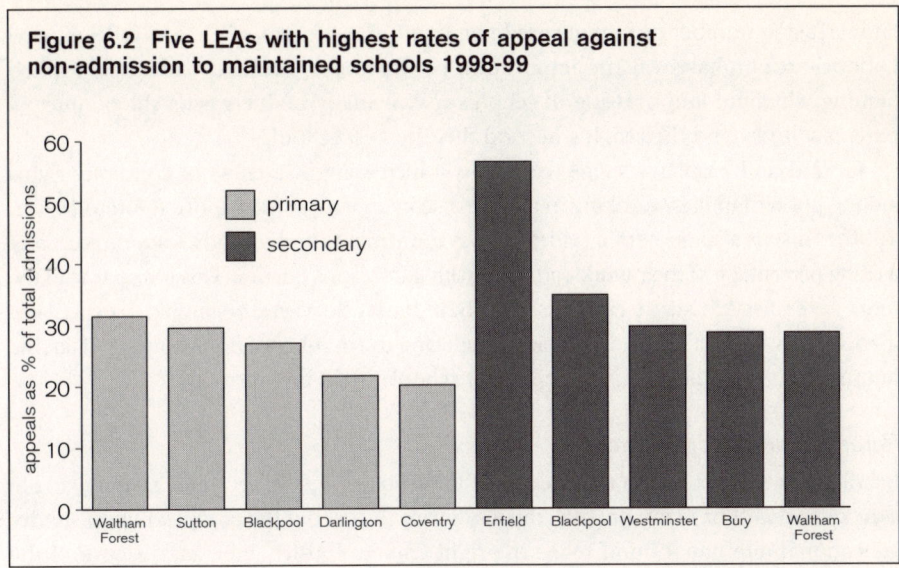

Figure 6.2 Five LEAs with highest rates of appeal against non-admission to maintained schools 1998-99

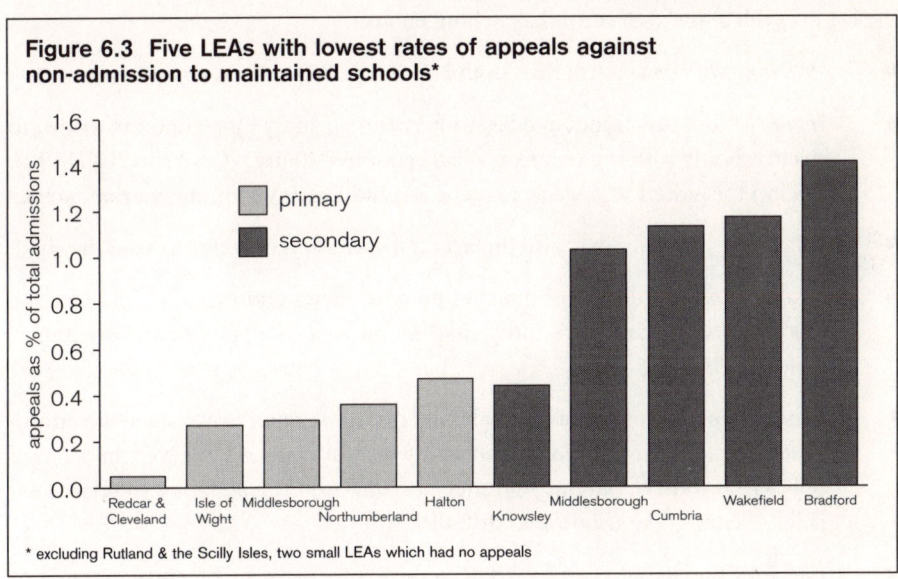

Figure 6.3 Five LEAs with lowest rates of appeals against non-admission to maintained schools*

* excluding Rutland & the Scilly Isles, two small LEAs which had no appeals

1994). Other studies demonstrate the class differentials in choice mentality; a school that is seen as 'unsuitable' for high SES parents is often the 'best available option' for others.

However, the evidence for this is often presumptuous; middle class parents could always manipulate systems effectively, and it may be that the more explicit system is gradually equalising the choices available to parents. There is growing evidence that an increasing number of parents are buying into the concept of choice. Indeed, New Labour's re-emphasis on the importance of education, coupled with their explicit naming, shaming and praising of schools may actually be increasing the number of parents who extend their sights beyond their nearest school.

Gorard and Fitz have suggested a slowly increasing awareness of consumer rights among poorer families, resulting in the increase in appeals shown above (Gorard & Fitz, 2000). There is also anecdotal evidence from some minority ethnic advocacy projects that a rising percentage of their workload deals with admissions queries. This is also true in the more generalist Advisory Centre for Education. It may be we are beginning to experience a 'trickle-down effect' of choice thinking, reducing the number of non-choosers. If so, the future pressures on popular and unpopular schools could be enormous.

Parents' criteria for choice

Echol's views on the choice strategies of Scottish parents have wider resonance. He concludes that 'For many parents, the task is not to sort out the complexities of sundry educational alternatives and make the right choice. Rather, their task is to find the nearest available 'suitable' school.' (Echols & Williams, 1992).

How is suitability decided? Six factors can be identified; the factors lower down the list may relate more to secondary school choice:

- *Proximity to home* is still the dominant or sole factor for many parents.

- *Intake* – Cookson argues in a large international study that 'choosers tended to select schools with higher mean socio-economic status.' (Cookson, 1994: 92). Within this criterion, race is a crucial but hidden driver in many urban areas.

- *Other parents' views* may also impact on the decision of where to send the child.

- *School ethos*, and how this matches parents' views and meets a child's needs. Within this, 'discipline' is often cited by parents as a key reason (Boulton & Coldron, 1996b).

- *Academic performance* has probably increased in significance since the advent of league tables, particularly in primary school choice. However, in a recent poll 81 per cent of parents said they had not used league tables to select their child's school (*The Guardian*, 29.2.00).

- *Children's views* are undoubtedly taken into account by most parents at primary to secondary transition (OECD, 1994; West *et al*, 1996).

One truism is worth mentioning; there is no doubt that, when a decision is made, a family's concerns are for the child, not the school or neighbourhood. Individual choice rarely takes external costs and benefits into account.

Effects on schools

School intake

This is the most contentious aspect of school choice research. Given our knowledge of the effects of peer groups on school performance, and particularly on the performance of low SES children, if parental choice is leading to social and racial polarisation between schools, then this would be a powerful argument for a policy shift (Feinstein, 1998). Such polarisation could also jeopardise the government's ambitions for more socially heterogeneous communities and schools.

Small scale studies in the UK and internationally have been virtually unanimous in agreeing that market forces, whether through parental choice of school or school choice of parent, have skewed intake (Gewirtz et al, 1995; Waslander & Thrupp, 1997; see also Gorard, 1999). This is supported by a recent study of 108 LEAs, which argues that 'the concentration of poor children within particular primary schools continues to increase.' (Howarth et al, 1999: 30). However, the recent findings of Gorard and Fitz give the only national picture of social stratification between schools. Using statistics from every school in England and Wales, they find that:

> ...overall segregation between schools has been declining since 1988 so that schools are generally becoming more mixed in their intakes over time. This is true of special educational needs and eligibility for, and take-up of, free school meals in both England and Wales, and at primary as well as secondary level (Gorard & Fitz, 2000: 1).

Schools are also becoming less racially segregated, as the intake of non-white students increases virtually everywhere. These results appear counter-intuitive, and the criteria are imperfect proxies that cannot cover all forms of social and economic variation. However, at the moment they provide by far the most accurate picture of the effects of school choice. In LEAs where segregation has increased, they argue that this is 'more likely to be due to social and demographic changes, coupled with local authority re-organisation and other more specifically local factors' (Gorard & Fitz, 2000).

However, the 'specifically local factors' are undoubtedly creating local predicaments, particularly in urban areas. Take, as an extreme example, the London borough of Islington. According to Gorard and Fitz, between-school segregation has decreased markedly there, and only one of its secondary schools is moving towards a less equal share of disadvantaged children. However, forty per cent of children living in the borough choose secondary schools outside the borough – a fact that undoubtedly damages Islington schools' performance (Islington Council Policy Committee, 2000). Cause and effect are difficult to unravel, yet the fact that Year 6s in Islington's primary schools in 1998 had a higher reading age than the Year Sevens in their secondary schools cannot be blamed on the quality of one year of schooling, but on the 'flight' of brighter children from the borough.

Choice may be having a positive effect on the heterogeneity of most schools' intakes, but the problems of choice are occurring at the extremes. At one end, oversubscribed schools that can, if they wish, choose their children in either overt or subtle ways and, through the use of the catchment area criterion, 'affect the structure of the prime housing market around Britain', according to a leading estate agent (in Worpole *et al*, 2000). At the other, where the conditions already exist for a school to be likely to face difficulties, motivated parents are moving their children away from that school. Schools with falling rolls face decreasing budgets and the extra burden of being forced to accept children excluded from other schools. There is also localised evidence that schools which are 'turned around' often do so at the expense of placing a neighbouring school in even greater difficulties, intake-wise. There can be little doubt that choice is partially responsible for the creation and continued existence of some 'sink schools' and 'sink boroughs'. The entrenched effects of residualisation can be clearly seen in the huge difficulties that are faced by many *Fresh Start* schools.

School behaviour
In forcing schools to face the discipline of the market, it was hoped that parent consumers would be able to shape school behaviour, raising attainment and creating genuine diversity between schools, as different schools competed for different parental niche markets.

Open enrolment and parental choice have undoubtedly impacted on the culture of all schools, yet it is highly disputable whether this has increased parental influence on them. Part of the reason is that schools are bank-like, in that once a choice is made, switching due to dissatisfaction is rare (although in the case of banks this is often due to apathy; moving schools has numerous external difficulties). In the bid to fill rolls and secure funds, schools therefore focus increasing attention on potential, not actual parents. In effect, this means more marketing, less consultation; more style, less substance.

Part of a school's presentational strategy may be to create a general image that may not serve the interests of all families. Although difficult to prove, the four-fold rise in exclusions during the 1990s, for instance, must in part be blamed on a combination of league tables and parental choice. As one headteacher has been quoted, '[exclusion] is about values and what the school stands for...and to show parents that the school does have standards.' (Munn, 1998: 4). And exclusion begins during the admissions process. Schools aim to optimise, not maximise their intake, and may therefore be changing their ethos to attract the parents of some children, and put off others.

If anything, the era of parental choice may have affected parental more than school behaviour. An example of this is the way in which some parents rediscover religion, and all its commitments, in order to secure a place for their child at a popular religious school. Voluntary aided schools are still permitted to use parental interviews as part of the selection procedure and, in spite of a tighter code of practice, there can be little doubt that covert selection continues. Anecdotal evidence from parents suggests that many schools take a flexible approach to whether a particular year group is 'full up'.

School diversity

This is an objective that parental choice has not really delivered. Parents are still not offered a large variety of school philosophies, learning styles, or curricular alternatives. This may be because parents' attitudes to schools are conservative, and they generally want similar things from any school. Yet running alongside the new right rhetoric of choice and diversity were the policies of standardisation and uniformity, which may have served to undermine any parental wishes for totally different types of school.

This dilemma is typified by the government's extension of specialist secondary schools and state funded religious schools. These schools appear successful and are popular, although it is difficult to separate the variable of extra resources. The freedom to select up to 10 per cent of pupils on the basis of aptitude is rarely used, and specialist schools are encouraged to see themselves as 'families of schools', ameliorating the effects of competition between schools. Yet as the OECD study on choice warned, although 'active diversification of educational supply' should be encouraged, centrally driven diversity 'creates the danger that schools will be assigned labels (such as technology school) that are not genuinely reflected in a change of ethos.' (OECD, 1994: 50).

Non-educational effects

School choice is an area where joined up thinking is clearly lacking. It exacerbates traffic problems, and through 'selection by catchment area' can hinder the goal, aimed for by this government, of socially mixed neighbourhoods.

More importantly, there may be a policy contradiction between school choice and the government's pronouncement on the importance of neighbourhood and community. If more children take the alternative option to their local school (and the specialist schools policy makes this inevitable), then their families may feel further dislocation from their neighbourhood. Schools can play an important part in preventing the total atomisation of neighbouring families. Choice makes this less likely. As Worpole argues,

> parental choice, longer school journeys, and the breakdown of spatial connections between home and school threaten the concept of 'neighbourhood' as the locus of the government's social policy. What happened to communitarianism with its emphasis on the school as the moral centre of the community? (Worpole *et al*, 2000)

Whitty *et al* also identify a clear dichotomy between the policies of choice and the policies to encourage collective neighbourhood action. Choice 'fosters a form of possessive individualism that is somewhat at odds with discourses that emphasise the 'stakeholder society' or the rebuilding of the social order.' (Whitty *et al*, 1998: 95). These discourses have outcomes that are hard to measure, but must nevertheless be valued.

Policy options

Gorard's conclusion that 'the advent of choice may be truly both less beneficial than some advocates suggest, and less harmful than some critics fear' appears correct (Gorard & Fitz, 2000:20). Evidence is still inconclusive as to whether two decades of choice have either produced consumer-responsive schools, or increased segregation.

However, there is also no doubt that, in certain pockets of neighbourhoods with certain characteristics, parental choice is breeding a collective panic; one that uses up irrational amounts of precious parental and school time and resources. It also seems likely that the current strains caused by choice demands will continue to increase. In the last year, there has been an emergence across the country of parents, whose children have been declined places at certain schools, setting up 'DIY schools' (*Daily Mail*, 2.10.1999; *Evening Standard*, 29.9.1999). Legal challenges to turned down admissions appeals could be launched through application of the Human Rights Act, for instance if arrangements have the effect of favouring children from a certain social class, which is unlikely to be objectively justifiable.

Part of the government's current strategy is to make choice unnecessary or less of an issue, through the drive for excellence in all schools. Yet even if attainment is raised across schools, this does not imply that inequalities between schools will be reduced; indeed, unlike in health, this is not a policy goal. Whether harmful or beneficial, it seems likely that choice will become increasingly relevant for an increasing number of families, and continue its permeation through the primary and possibly pre-school sectors.

The DfEE has claimed that 'if parents were given clear information they could make a better assessment of their chances. Maybe then they would get a school they would like.'[2] Yet increasing the information obligations on schools would not satisfy a rising demand for choice to be met.

Can choice be made fairer?

The removal of parental choice as a policy goal is neither a viable nor a desirable option. But policies are needed to ameliorate some of the injustices caused by choice in extreme situations. Put simply, choice needs to be rendered more equitable for both families and schools.

One option was originally proposed by the National Commission on Education (National Commission on Education, 1993). A local admissions authority should be able to ringfence a percentage of every school's intake. The Commission recommended ten per cent, but this may need to be larger to be effective. This percentage could be used for:

- children whose parents cannot afford to move into the catchment area of a popular school. Free travel would need to be provided by the admissions authority
- children who have been excluded or are at risk of exclusion, thus spreading the responsibilities for disaffected pupils between schools
- 'mobile' children, especially refugees and those who are transient through family breakdown or passing through the care system

After this percentage, parental choice would have primacy, and admissions criteria would be, within the current guidelines, at a school's discretion. A necessary legislative change would be that schools could no longer be their own admissions authorities. Instead, some of this power would need to be retained within an LEA or alternative supra-school admissions authority. It should be noted that this ringfencing would be used at an admissions authority's discretion; in many parts of the country, this would be totally unnecessary. Local variation in admissions procedures should be encouraged, as should co-operation between neighbouring Authorities.

Another option, far more radical, has recently been proposed by Harry Brighouse, to 'enhance social justice in education by helping disadvantaged parents to choose good schools for their children' (*The Independent*, 8.6.2000; Brighouse, 2000). This would involve selection by a lottery of all those within a large catchment area, giving financial incentives to encourage schools to attract a social mix of applicants. The budget constraints of low-income families would again be offset by free travel.

Both of these options would probably increase the number of children who did not attend their most local school. But this may be inevitable anyway in the current system. If so, these options and alternative models should be considered, and space should be created for local experimentation and variation. A pre-requisite for any change of policy must be consultation with parents and pupils.

Can choice be increased?

Should the state attempt to increase the range of school choices? If this was seen as desirable, it may have no options other than to open the education market to the private and voluntary sectors, who may be more prepared to bear the costs and risks of surplus places. Although vouchers are unwieldy and unlikely to be repeated, it is not beyond belief that per-capita funding could be extended to any school, private public or voluntary. As long as this was done with three provisos, such a policy might not conflict with social justice goals. These are:

- Schools would not be allowed to ask parents to pay 'top up fees'
- All schools involved would be part of the admissions authorities described above
- Relaxed quality assurance mechanisms would be put in place

Opening up the education system in this way may be the only way to drive in true choice and bottom-up diversity, especially if quality assurance mechanisms are more relaxed for such schools. This may require a loosening up of nationally defined success criteria, for instance the requirement to teach the national curriculum. The aim would not only be to bring in the private sector, but also to offer opportunities to small schools, or even parent-run schools with alternative educational philosophies.

The state's reluctance to support such schools comes from two sources. Financially, the creation of such schools could be costly, as they are likely to be small, and could undermine the planning and organisation of school places. Philosophically, giving parents encouragement to run a school and teach a curriculum as they determine would run against the prevailing educational vein of centralised control of values, curriculum and pedagogy.

The concept may form a future strand of the already occurring blurring of private and public sectors. There are international precedents. In The Netherlands, independent schools are fully state-subsidised, and two thirds of pupils attend independently controlled establishments, many of which were established by parents. And in Denmark, the state subsidises 85 per cent of the costs of private schools. Eleven per cent of children attend such schools.

Although the theoretical questions over whether parents and others should be given the opportunity to create new schools are interesting, the argument may seem too peripheral to mainstream educational debate. Even if legislation changed, as proposed by the Conservatives, a tiny minority of parents would have the will, resources or time to undertake such a project. However, as the ultimate from of parental choice and self-governance, the idea of state subsidised community-run schools demands long term consideration, not as the Conservative solution for failing schools, but as an idea with huge social capital and social justice possibilities.

Conclusion

This chapter offers no policy conclusions beyond a call for visionary thinking about admissions, and a long-term outlook on the possible effects of an increasing parental demand for their choices to be met. Admissions policies may need further local variation and experimentation, even if some LEAs initiate changes that may seem unpalatable. A clear values question of whether the policy goal should be choice-driven or equity-driven needs to be debated. A second question remains whether the system should actively encourage a range of choices, through school diversity, or espouse the vision that the local choice should be the best choice. Given the importance of the idea of neighbourhood in the government's thinking on community and social capital, it seems logical that pupils and parents should be encouraged to develop some kinds of links with their most local school. However, this may not mean full time attendance at that school. As schools develop specialisms and stay open for longer, ties could be developed through one particular subject (at secondary level) or out of hours learning.

However, the most important policy considerations of choice stem not from what it has done, but what it has not done. In particular, it has not increased parental influence over the nature and content of schools. The power of exit is proving a poor substitute for the power of voice.

Endnotes

1 All of these statistics predate the new admissions framework introduced by the 1998 School Standards and Framework Act.
2 Garner, S in *TES*, 2.7.99

7. Parental voice

> *The real job of re-knitting the social fabric has to begin where the threads start. That means getting more people involved in politics at the local level. There are too many people in positions of authority who are not leading, and too many at grass roots resigned to the way things are.* (Robert Reich, 1998)

Of all the proposals relating to parents in *Excellence in Schools*, the suggestion that 'parents should have a greater say in the way schools are run' remains the least developed (DfEE, 1997b: 55). Though much of the legislation and initiatives described in this report are transforming home-school relationships, power relations between education services and their users appear, except in extreme cases, to have remained remarkably static. Consumer choice policies in particular have not led to, and may even have militated against, increased parental influence over school policies and philosophies. As the Social Exclusion Unit's recent *Schools Plus* report concluded, 'the growing importance of a role for parents as individual consumers has inevitably created tensions with schools' traditional role as servants of a wider community interest.' (Social Exclusion Unit, 2000: 84).

Currently, parents' rights in the UK are represented entirely in terms of the rights of individual parents. Their views are often obtained as aggregates of these; their dealings with schools are as (relatively) powerless individuals versus powerful collective organisations; Parent Teacher Associations are the exceptions that prove the rule because they are largely toothless and optional.

The central argument of this chapter is that *our education system should begin to experiment with new ways to give parents collective influences over education decision making*. Although the opportunity costs need to be carefully evaluated, the benefits could be multi-dimensional.

Justifications for voice

Apart from the obvious, right-based argument that every decision making process should take into account the opinions of all those affected by a decision, the following justifications exist:

Parental voice can raise a school's quality

This justification is disputable. Although most successful schools seem to have more developed forms of democratic engagement with parents than legislation demands, there is also evidence at the other extreme of parental voice becoming loudest when a 'failing' school is threatened with closure. There is no guarantee that parental voice will aid or even support nationally defined success criteria. But voice can have positive unintended outcomes. Parental involvement in decisions over how schools are run is a largely untapped resource, which has the potential to energise parental involvement in all the other areas that this report has described.

Parental voice can positively harness parental discontent

There is some consensus that clients of all services have become increasingly prepared to challenge what Giddens describes as 'expert systems' (Giddens, 1991). This is possibly less true for education than any other service. Choice legislation may prove to have been a two-decade release valve for these challenges, yet one which may soon clog up, due to unmet demand. If so, how will this voice express itself? Vincent and Martin give a useful typology of parental action:

- *Silence* (inaction, non-articulation, waiting and seeing)
- *Informal conversation* (engaging with the system)
- *Formal deliberation* (writing or formally meeting)
- *Storming* (protesting against the system)
- *By-pass* (going round the system; making own arrangements)
- *Exit* (abandoning the system; child leaves the school) (Vincent *et al*, 2000)

Since the advent of compulsory education, silence has probably been the dominant type of 'action'. Unless the education system improves its mechanisms for informal conversation and formal deliberation, it is likely that parental use of storming, by-pass and exit strategies will continue to grow. The Human Rights Act, which gives parents and children new rights to obtain the education of their choice, may add legal weight to the storming and exit processes.

Parental voice can build trust and social capital

Parental voice appears to be the missing link in the government's semi-articulated vision of parents as school citizens and schools as citizen-creating institutions. Granting influence over decision making gives users additional rights and responsibilities. If effective, it can foster deeper attachments between schools and families, and even restore popular faith in the value of wider democratic participation. Alexander writes that 'schools must become democratic learning communities in which the experience of participation, responsibility and real power are as much part of learning as instruction.' (Alexander, 2000: 1). This vision should equally apply to pupils, parents and staff.

Barriers and concerns

School and teacher attitudes

Although teachers are generally positive about parents' involvement as supporters, they are clearly concerned by an increase in 'parent power'. In the IPPR/ATL survey, 74 per cent of teachers disagreed with the statement 'parents should have a greater say in the way schools are run.'. Within the current perception of a top-down agenda, there is a feeling that parental voice could further squeeze teacher autonomy and professionalism. Yet parental participation can help to empower a whole school community. The trade off may not be between teacher and parent power, but between national prescription and school autonomy.

However, given current teacher attitudes and morale, the recommendations below should come with the following proviso: *Schools should be encouraged but not coerced into increasing parental involvement in decision making.* Such involvement can promote trust between parents and teachers; such trust is a prerequisite for the building of social capital between schools and all their stakeholders.

At the same time, parents' rights to voice should not fall victim to 'professional capture'. Current Parent Teacher Associations are ineffective at articulating parental voice. Joint forums often dampen a distinct parental voice. Therefore, *space should be found at all levels for parent-only discussions and bodies. At times, it may be necessary to take the 'T' out of the PTA.*

Parental attitudes

Two concerns arise: one is that parents naturally prioritise their own child's needs over a school's. The other is that parents have unequal levels of skills and capital to utilise participatory structures. As a result, any transfer of power to parents can lead to a tyranny of an articulate and already advantaged minority.

The first concern appears, in practice, to be unwarranted. Research has shown that parents who do enter a school's decision making sphere, whether through governing bodies or other mechanisms, can be relatively neutral, and be involved in deliberations about wider systems and policy issues. Sociologists talk of 'the strength of weak ties', whereby heterogeneous groups of individuals can be far more outward looking and objective than groups with stronger bonds and associations (Granovetter, 1973: 1360-80). This is a thesis that demands to be tested.

The second, however, is more worrying. Research shows that parents who are currently involved in such decision making are overwhelmingly middle class (Deem *et al*, 1995). Yet this is true for all democratic structures, and is not in itself a reason to prevent voice. Another proviso emerges: *Any strategy to encourage parental participation in decision making must aim to be inclusive and deliberately target groups that are likely to be underrepresented, and reflect the diversity of families in any school.*

A striking omission from the Social Exclusion Unit's 'Schools Plus' report was any call for an increase in parental voice in schools in disadvantaged areas. Expertise found outside the education system, for instance from the Citizens' Organising Foundation, or the Black advocacy organisations, needs to be sought.

Insufficient parental time/interest

There is an oft-expressed view that it is difficult enough for many parents to involve themselves in their own child's learning, let alone become embroiled in the details of school budgets or planning. Early research into the Home-School Agreement consultation processes appears to confirm this (Ouston *et al*, 2000). Many headteachers argue that the energy required to organise consultation often gives a poor rate of return. Time will be a constant barrier to parental participation, but, again, this should not prevent experimentation. New technology needs to be used to maximise involvement, and schools should think seriously about the timing, location and format of all participation opportunities. Childcare facilities should be the norm at all meetings. Even the House of Commons is slowly waking up to the view that, in the 21st century, a forum with no crèche is no forum at all.

The rest of this chapter will chart existing mechanisms and suggest new possibilities at school, local and national levels. All of the proposals are made with one underlying assumption – *if the government's current strategies are successful, they have committed themselves to eroding the levels of central interventions on a school-by-school basis. Thus, as targets are met, the autonomy of nearly all schools should grow. Therefore, increases in 'parent power' should occur simultaneously with increases in 'pupil power' and 'teacher power'.* Conflicts will be inevitable, but such conflict could be a precondition for progress.

Decision-making at school level

Governing bodies

The quality of governing bodies varies as much as the quality of schools, although it often appears that governing bodies are least effective where they are most needed. However, there is growing consensus that governing bodies are proving an inadequate vehicle for the proper consideration of parental views.

This is partly because this has never been their explicit role. Leadbeater is wrong in claiming that 'with parents electing governors, the head is accountable to a parents' mutual.' (Leadbeater, 1999). Although parental representation on governing bodies has risen four times since the 1980 Education Act, parent governors still do not form a majority on governing bodies. Besides, it has never been the remit of elected parent governors to represent the interests of all parents.

The Audit Commission described a purpose of governing bodies as 'making sure that parents are kept informed about what is happening in the school and that their views are taken into account', not representing their views (Audit Commission & Oftsed, 1995: 4). Ofsted advises that governing bodies of schools in Special Measures should help schools by 'keeping parents informed about how the school is improving.' (Ofsted, 1997: 15). Again, this implies information without participation.

The changed role of governing bodies is also partly responsible. Legislation from Local Management of Schools onwards has forced governing bodies to concentrate on their managerial role at the expense of genuine governance, the determining of a school's individual ethos. New responsibilities on governing bodies for target setting, performance management, as well as the increased financial delegation to schools, is leading them further to prioritise their allocative role over their authoritative role. The local politics of education has been increasingly reduced to an economics. The 1998 School Standards and Framework Act (S38.(2)) stated that 'the governing body shall conduct the school with a view to promoting high standards of educational achievement at the school', but, as yet, there is no evidence that governing bodies have been liberated by recent legislation. In this process, parent governors appear to have been marginalised by professional voices, or co-opted into using managerial skills such as accounting, rather than shaping a school's direction (Deem *et al*, 1995; Creese *et al*, 1999; NAGM survey, in *TES*, 11.6.99).

The common experience of the annual governors' report and meeting to parents appears to crystallise the inability of governing bodies to engage with parent bodies. In theory, the meetings have clout – a governing body must allow parents to vote on any resolutions put forward at the meeting. If the number of parents attending is at least 20 per cent of the number of pupils at the school, then any resolution passed is regarded as valid, and the governing body is formally required to consider it. Halpin describes the average meeting as a lost opportunity: 'stultifyingly boring, poorly attended and inhibiting of discussion.' (Halpin, 1999 ; Hinds *et al*, 1992). As always, excellent practice exists; many schools have improved attendance by combining the meeting with a social event. Yet the report and meeting typify the current one-way information process between governing bodies and parent bodies. As the DfEE has argued against the views of the Education and Employment Select committee, these meetings need transformation, not abolition.

Recent recommendations from the Select Committee and the Better Regulation Task Force may help to ease governor overload (House of Commons, 1999; Better Regulation Task Force, 2000). But the streamlining of their functions will still only assist the input of parent governors, not necessarily all parents. Parents need new access routes to school decision making.

Although there have been a few calls for governing bodies to be abolished, this is unlikely to occur in the near future. Thus the alternatives described and suggested below will need to be bolted onto rather than bypass current systems of governance.

Where schools do experiment with new forms of governance, as is likely to happen with City Academies and other initiatives, these schools should not just be encouraged but required to create structures that increase parental participation. Many US Charter Schools provide excellent role models.

Alternative inputs

There is no single way to improve and increase parental voice. For some schools, opening up an informal dialogue for parents to feed in comments and suggestions may be sufficient. Some may take the route of innovative whole school consultation. Others may prefer to create structures for more formal, representative participation. What is needed is the opportunity to take risks. *Schools should be encouraged to experiment with new forms of parental involvement in decision making. A strand of the DfEE's Standards Fund should be dedicated to 'parental participation', to give schools the opportunity to bid for resources to do this.*

Three decision making spheres can be identified:

- consumer issues, for instance over the amount of homework
- strategy issues, for instance over the types of teaching and learning taking place
- management issues, for instance budgets

Although schools should have the freedom to deliberate with parents over all these issues, parents seem far more willing to engage themselves with consumer and strategy issues than those relating to day to day management.

Input through parents' forums

Current Parent Teacher Associations rarely move beyond the parents-as-supporters model of involvement. Parents' forums or councils have an explicit and challenging role in questioning and shaping school policies. In opposition, the Labour Party's *Charter for Parents* argued for 'formal participation at the class and school level, set within a legislative framework' (Straw, 1991: 4). The councils and forums described below are mainly advisory, with no statutory decision making powers.

Box 7.1 Parents Forums: International examples[2]

Although structures of school governance and levels of school and local autonomy differ widely between countries, it is striking that nearly every European country and OECD country has some form of parent's forum at school level.

Canada Virtually every school now has a *Parent Committee*. Although the role is mainly advisory, in certain states, parents have a degree of control over the curriculum and recruitment.

Denmark The views of parents' class councils, that meet at least termly with the class teacher, feed directly into Skolenoevns (school boards), although classroom practices and teaching methods are explicitly outside their remits.

France Each school has a *conseil de classe*. The Head chooses representatives from a list provided by the parents' association.

Germany There is a growing trend for parents' councils at Land (federal state) and school level, with a mainly advisory role. In some Länder, schools are obliged to consider any council's recommendations.

Netherlands The responsibilities of the *medezeggenschapsraad* (compulsory school forums for parents, teachers & pupils) have been widened, so that some policy decisions need to be verified by the forum.

Sweden Some School Councils have a veto over a head's decisions.

Box 7.2 Parents' Forums: UK examples

Any forums to involve parents in policy decisions in the UK have been truly bottom-up; beyond the annual meeting, governing bodies have no rights or duties to consult parents beyond the annual meeting. Yet it is worth remembering that parent governors themselves were a bottom-up initiative, introduced by Sheffield schools in 1970. The examples below are rare, although many secondary schools organise parents' forums around year groups.

In *Warwickshire*, three schools have been 'named and acclaimed' for consultation with parents:
- *Woodloes Junior School* has organised termly parents' forums, initially to review communication strategies, but also to give parents a more general voice about school policies.
- *Nathaniel Newton Infant School* holds an open half termly coffee morning to discuss anything related to the school. As a result, the school reviewed its reporting strategy. Parents are also involved in constructing the school's annual development plan.
- *Claverdon Primary School* used the following procedure to consult over its homework policy:
  - Working party, including parents
  - Involving pupils through councils and assemblies
  - Writing draft, and sending it for consultation
  - Inviting every tenth name on register to meet to 'fine tune' the policy (Warwickshire County Council, 1999)

> *Suffolk LEA parental partnership* has extended its role beyond working with parents of children with SEN, holds workshops for parents to help schools identify aspects of home-school policies that are working well and aspects that could be improved.
>
> In many *supplementary and mother-tongue schools*, parents form 50 per cent of the management committee (see appendix 3).
>
> At *Melbourn Village College* in Cambridge, a series of initiatives were developed to involve parents in the school's development. In small groups parents were invited to discuss 'What makes a good school?'. A 'Parents as Co-educators' (PACE) group was formed, consisting of staff, students, governors and parents. This group took forward consultation for the college's home-school agreement. Positive outcomes of the initiative have been improvements in the level of participation and quality of communications and changes in the college culture (Cambridgshire County Council, 1999).
>
> *PTA Devon* has initiated an *Investors in Parents* Research Project. It aims to encourages parents to take responsibility for driving forward initiatives in school communities that open new avenues of opportunity for parents wanting to participate in their children's learning and their own learning. Parents' Action Teams have been established in nine secondary and six primary schools. Their remit varies between schools, but includes 'consultation and decision making' (DeRijke, 2000).

There are many differences between types of parental forums; some are parents-only, others involve equal numbers of parents and teachers. Subjects for discussion also vary; some include the traditional PTA role, others focus specifically on policy. A third difference is whether such forums are based at class level, school level or both. Research evidence is also needed, especially from Europe, as to which mechanisms are most effective and are most sustainable, and how such structures impact on a school's culture.

Input into the curriculum

The idea of a national curriculum is now relatively uncontroversial and particularly popular with parents. Yet when asked, parents tend to agree that they would like some say over what is taught in schools. Space for schools to determine some elements of their curricula is being squeezed by time pressures – the first review of the national curriculum counselled that around twenty per cent of time at key stages One to Three should be for use at the discretion of the school, but overload effectively rendered this impossible. The recent National Curriculum review aimed for less prescription and more flexibility, without revisiting the 20 per cent concept. Future curriculum changes are likely to be incremental, and should add to existing flexibilities. There may soon be possibilities for schools to enjoy a genuine 'light touch' curriculum, parts of which could be determined by parents and pupils.

This has international precedents; in Israel, 25 per cent of every school's curriculum is determined through consultation with parents (Katz, 1997). Before its break up, the Soviet Union experimented with a portion of per-capita funding that was under parental authority. Parents could determine what their child's school should spend that money on, and thus have a degree of control over curricular priorities. This led to a rise in business studies and non-Russian languages (Glenn, 1995; Heyneman, 1997).

The Soviet experiment may be too radical to gain national consideration, although it would be fascinating if any school was confident enough to try it. Two possibilities are worth considering: one is that *future changes to the National Curriculum should aim to ensure that a percentage of every school's time is ringfenced, to be used at a school's discretion in consultation with all education stakeholders*. This time could be permeated throughout the year, or be concentrated into, say, one half term. This could give schools real diversity, providing a window for parents to bring hidden skills and passions into schools.

Another, more immediate opportunity is provided by the introduction of citizenship education as optional for primary schools and, from 2002, statutory for secondary schools. Although there is some guidance, there is, commendably, space for schools to determine their own content, and prioritise their values. This is an ideal chance for schools to consult with, and as a result, involve parents in the formulation and delivery of citizenship education (see Pearce & Hallgarten, 2000).

Input through inspections

The Ofsted process has undoubtedly given parents a rich source of information, but this has generally been used to inform parental choice, not voice. Parental responses to Ofsted inspections are generally positive, although reports could undoubtedly be simplified (this is already occurring with the summary documents) (Tabberer, 1995). Of greater concern is the extent to which parents truly contribute to the assessment of a school's performance. Although parents are consulted during an inspection through a questionnaire, a whole school meeting, and, if requested, individual meetings, these views are included separately in reports, and do not seem to be embedded into the inspection process. Research has also shown that the lay inspector, whose purpose is partly to liaise with parents, has become increasingly professionalised and distant (Hustler in *TES*, 26.9.97).

Although the purpose of inspection is to provide an external voice, it should consider the following options to allow parents to play a fuller part in the deliberations:

- *deliberative consultation using focus groups, panels or other innovative methods*
- *an additional parents meeting after the inspection has been finished but before the final report has been written, so that parents are consulted on a 'first draft'*

A final option to increase parental involvement in the inspection process stems from the concept of schools' self-evaluation (MacBeath, 1999). In this system, which has been widely piloted in various forms throughout the world, a school effectively asks itself how well it is doing, measuring itself against success criteria that it has set and has ownership of. A whole school community is involved in the process, and the process itself has been found to energise parental involvement in all areas of school life. If done rigorously, self-evaluation is anything but a soft option. Advocates argue that the role of the external inspection should be reduced to inspecting how well a school is evaluating itself. The DfEE, local authorities and even Ofsted itself are showing increasing enthusiasm for the idea of self-evaluation, although they see it as an addition, not an alternative to external inspection. As such systems are implemented, it is crucial that the parental voice is central to the process.

Input through appraisal

It seems logical that parents, like pupils, should have some input into the appraisal of a teacher's performance. The Green Paper on teaching reforms asserted that 'feedback from pupils, parents and governors may also be relevant and informative.' (DfEE, 1998d: 10). What makes the suggestion controversial is the new link between appraisal and pay as part of the new performance management regime, to be implemented from September. Teachers are understandably sceptical of the idea that the prejudices of parents could affect their pay. In IPPR's survey, 77 per cent of teachers disagreed that 'the appraisal process should take the views of parents into account'.

It remains to be seen whether headteachers, governors and external assessors consult parents over whether individual teachers should cross the pay threshold. However, as the system is ironed out, and hopefully gains the support of the teaching profession, *the government should consider whether at a later stage consultation with parents should have a statutory role in the performance management process.*

Decision-making at local level

> Councils decide on priorities in consultation with their communities and other partners, build[ing] consensus on what needs to be achieved...these priorities will flow from engagement with the wider community...an authority...needs to know what local people think (DETR, 1998b: 36).

In response to the new agenda set out in the Local Government White Paper, Local Education Authorities appear to be waking up to the idea of local consultation at precisely the time when there is less and less to consult over. Their responsibilities and funding are being devolved, centralised, or outsourced. Consultation, especially in boroughs where many parents are choosing to send their children elsewhere, may prove to be too little, too late.

Some LEAs have already used innovative forms of consultation over certain issues. Wigan employed citizens' juries to assist deliberations over a switch to a new school year pattern. Consultation over the outsourcing of Kings' Manor School in Guildford involved genuine dialogue with parents. However, although many Authorities have consultative groups, few are parent-only or parent-majority, so many are susceptible to capture from teachers and LEA officers. A 1994 RISE survey found that 'a small minority of LEAs of all political persuasions are enthusiastic supporters of parental involvement.' (O'Connor, 1994: 29).

Recent developments are not encouraging. One of the rationales behind Education Development Plans is to 'make LEAs publicly accountable to schools, parents and the local community for their role in raising standards.' (DfEE, 1998e: 3). Yet there is little evidence of active engagement of parents in the formulation or evaluation of education development plans or any other LEA plans; nor do these plans mention new opportunities for local consultation. As an exception, Enfield has a local parents' council to contribute to and monitor the plan.

At least two parent governor representatives now sit on every LEA's education committee. In some cases, as many as five have been appointed. In an LEA that has changed its political structures in advance of new legislation, for instance to include 'cabinet style' structures, parent governor representatives have a role on the overview and scrutiny committees. These committees will be able to hold the executive to account, monitor policy implementation and propose new policies. Time will tell how effective their role will be.

Again, England is the European exception; virtually every other EU country has a statutory duty to consult with established parents' bodies at the local level (Eurydice, 1997). This may reflect wider issues about popular and national attitudes to local democracy. Given the likely impact of the White Paper on school funding, it may also be too late to address this deficiency; there could soon be little to consult about. Yet if LEAs had acted earlier to involve parents in deliberative decision making, their future might now be less tenuous.

Education Action Zones

> Whether you are a parent or a business, a headteacher, a teacher or a school governor, a voluntary organisation or an LEA, this is your chance to get involved in applying to set up an Education Action Zone. (DfEE, 1999c).

Touted as 'dynamic frameworks' for partnerships, many Education Action Zones are promoting family involvement in learning through a variety of innovate projects. However, there is as yet no clear evidence that the current seventy three zones are exploring innovative methods of involving parents in decision making, through consultation or otherwise. Parents have played virtually no part in setting up any of the EAZs. No parents' organisations are listed as zone partners. Although the

Statutory Instruments for EAZs includes parent representatives in virtually every zone's forum, there is evidence that parent representatives have not been appointed to some of the forums. In one zone forum, an additional headteacher has been appointed to represent parents' interests! With forum membership often exceeding 50 and rising in one case to 82, the potential to exercise 'parent power' through the forum is limited. In addition, all forums have a smaller 'executive group' where major decisions appear to be taken and from which parents tend to be excluded.

This is especially ironic, considering that a central strand of almost all zones is to increase parental involvement in their children's learning and schools. Although many zones are using innovative methods to do this, parents are generally not being consulted on *how* they would like to be involved. If EAZs fail to achieve their objectives, this could be a key reason.

Why has this been neglected? EAZs are in areas of high deprivation, where there are many barriers to parental involvement and engagement. There seems to be an underlying perception that to involve such parents in decision making about their involvement or the zone generally is like trying to run before they can walk. IPPR's consultation with parents in the Wednesbury EAZ (see appendix 2) appears to refute this. In particular, the focus groups revealed a high level of support for the creation of a parents' network across schools, an idea that the zone is pursuing. Leicester EAZ has also consulted widely with parents.

If there is to be a third round of EAZs, *bids should show a much greater commitment to and evidence of consultation with parents, teachers and pupils. The 'Excellence in Cities' and 'city academy' initiatives should also learn from the experiences of EAZs*. Crouch's question is pertinent: 'Can universalist social policy develop strategies for improving the participative skills of the disadvantaged, rather than use them as an excuse for retreating behind inaccessible bureaucracy?' (Crouch, 1999: 20). As Halpin argues, democratic association is especially important in the quest to create genuinely inclusive schooling (Halpin, 1998).

Decision-making at the national level

More than ever before, the current Government has sought to consult all education stakeholders about national policy. The multi-faceted consultation over *Excellence in Schools* brought over 3,500 responses from parents (Cabinet Office, 1999). This is a relatively small number, but still demonstrates their commitment. A network has been established to support parent governor representatives nationally. The network will also be used by Ministers as one channel of communication with parents, with occasional feedback sought on consultation proposals. More can always be done; for instance the parents' centre on the DfEE's website has yet to be used as a consultative mechanism. Yet progress has been made. Portugal's lead could be followed, where an agreement has been signed between the Confederation of Parents Associations and the Ministry of Education, committing the government to 'the participation of parents in the definition of educational policy' (Stoer & Cortesao, 1999: 28).

There is one missing link; parents are still not represented by a single body at the national level. Yet again, most countries of Europe have such a body. The arguments against the creation of such a body are limp. Of course, parents are a heterogeneous group, and cannot be truly represented by a few individuals. The same could be said for virtually every national organisation. This is why such a body would need to have a clear research function, to ensure that it represents the views of all parents.

The government should seek to create a National Parents' Council. As with the General Teaching Council, the body would be consulted about all initiatives. Unlike the GTC, it would not ask for a registration fee, which could skew membership. Parents would vote for some representatives and others would come from existing bodies, for instance the NCPTA and National Governors' Council. Clearly, the details need to be thought through, and international experiences need to be learnt from. Yet the idea needs urgent exploration. A National Parents' Council could stimulate and support school-based participation. The formation of a National Parent's Council in Ireland in 1995 has sent ripples of increased parental participation throughout their school system.

Conclusion

This report has been written against a backdrop that the future of publicly provided education may be under threat. Privately managed schools, local authority and other educational services are growing, mainly in areas where the public sector is perceived to have failed.

One of the main arguments used to justify the private sector's involvement in education is that only the private sector can be truly accountable and responsive to the demands of parents. Although this report has remained neutral on the private/public debate, part of its aim has been to show that, with the right support, policies and attitudes, the public sector is capable of providing an educational service with equal responsiveness and accountability. This can occur not through the incentives and threats of market mechanisms, but out of mutual self-interest. Users, both pupils and parents, can be empowered, and a publicly funded and provided service thus becomes an efficient, client-driven driver of change. Such a public would not crowd out civil society, but be a key catalyst for its renewal. Democracy is not necessarily an enemy of efficiency.

With the exception of Japan, England and Wales have probably the least developed mechanisms for parental involvement in decision making of any other OECD or EU country. Many of the reasons for this are beyond the clutches of the education system, yet schools and wider educational structures may still provide the solution.

The recommendations made in this chapter are for consideration at *all levels*:

- Our education system should begin to experiment with new ways to give parents collective influences over education decision making.
- If the government's current strategies are successful, they have committed themselves to eroding the levels of central interventions on a school-by-school basis. Thus, as targets are met, the autonomy of nearly all schools should grow. Therefore, increases in 'parent power' should occur simultaneously with increases in 'pupil power' and 'teacher power'.
- Space should be found at all levels for parent-only discussions and bodies. At times, it may be necessary to take the 'T' out of the PTA.
- Any strategy to encourage parental participation in decision making must aim to be inclusive and deliberately target groups that are likely to be underrepresented, and reflect the diversity of families in any school.
- Where schools do experiment with new forms of governance, as is likely to happen with City Academies and other initiatives, these schools should not just be encouraged but required to create structures that increase parental participation.
- Schools should be encouraged but not coerced to experiment with new forms of parental involvement in decision making. A strand of the DfEE's Standards Fund should be dedicated to 'parental participation', to give schools the opportunity to bid for resources to do this. Examples could include class councils, year forums, or steering groups on certain issues.
- Future changes to the National Curriculum should aim to ensure that a percentage of every school's time is ringfenced, to be used at a school's discretion in consultation with all education stakeholders.
- Ofsted should consider the following options to allow parents to play a fuller part in the deliberations:
  - deliberative consultation using focus groups, panels or other innovative methods
  - an additional parents meeting after the inspection has been finished but before the final report has been written, so that parents are consulted on a 'first draft'
- The government should consider whether at a later stage consultation with parents should have a statutory role in the performance management process.

- If there is to be a third round of EAZs, bids should show a much greater commitment to and evidence of consultation with parents, teachers and pupils. The 'Excellence in Cities' and 'city academy' initiatives should also learn from the experiences of EAZs.

- The government should seek to create a National Parents' Council.

Research evidence is also needed, especially from Europe, as to which mechanisms are most effective and are most sustainable, and how such structures impact on a school's culture.

Potential problems with such an agenda are enormous, but schools need to be given the confidence to take risks. The problem is that, without a massive cultural shift, many schools and teachers will be obstructive in taking forward such an agenda. But the agenda itself has the potential to bring about such whole-school change. Voice is the unused bandwidth of parental involvement in their children's learning.

Endnotes

1   An NFER study by Keys W and Fernandes C (1990: 33) revealed that:
    - 44 per cent of Governors had degree of professional qualification.
    - 18 per cent were employed in industry or commerce
    - 39 per cent were employed in education/training
    - a very low proportion were from manual occupations
    - one per cent were from ethnic minorities
2   All of these examples are taken from Euridyce (1997) and OECD (1997) *Parents as Partners in Schooling* London: OECD
3   Many of the ideas here were contained in the Scottish Consumer Council (2000) report.

8. A framework for whole-school change

A central vision of this report, set out in the introduction, is that policies need to be constructed to make schools more family-like, rather than families more school-like. Such a vision can be assisted but not realised by the recommendations made so far in this report, What is required is that schools undergo dynamic cultural change. This type of change will not be achieved through a new homework policy, or a parent volunteer scheme, or even a home school agreement. Whole school change requires whole school systems thinking.

This concluding chapter does not revisit existing recommendations. Instead, it reviews four locations where whole school change can be enabled: national level; local level; school level, and finally parents themselves.

National level

This report has stressed throughout that *the national role in supporting home-school relationships should be an enabling one.* National awareness campaigns for parents, such as the National Year of Reading, can be effective in both encouraging parental support for their children's learning and schools. The new parents' guide to the National Curriculum and associated *Learning Journey* literature should assist with this. Funding streams and training requirements can also influence attitudes and practice. There will always be scope at the national level for general, targeted intervention in underachieving schools that may impact on home-school relationships. However, specific, universal initiatives to encourage schools to improve home-school links, such as prescriptive obligations on information, may have reached critical mass. Further legislation on schools in the home-school field could follow the law of diminishing or even negative returns. Aside from training, discussed below, the most important way that schools can be supported at the national level to improve relationships with parents is to encourage innovation, through targeted resources and greater 'freedom to take risks' in all areas of school life. This report has suggested several funding streams that the DfEE could use to achieve this. *A more holistic approach would be to develop an 'investors in parents' programme, or build similar criteria into any school's 'investors in people' status.*

Local level

Local Education Authorities have been at the vanguard of many positive home-school developments, particularly in the SEN field. They have been especially effective at working in concert with voluntary organisations and the Further Education sector, for instance to generate family learning opportunities. Ofsted's inspection reports of

Authorities rarely mention their work with parents; this is a serious weakness in the inspection process.

In the current climate of fear over further diminishing of their responsibilities and resources, LEAs appear to be focussing on short-term support and pressure on schools. Much excellent work is continuing, but much of the innovation and experimentation of old seems to be drying up. A reading of Education Development Plans reveals a huge degree of uniformity, possibly caused by the undermining of local priorities by central prescription. Authorities whose futures as service providers are threatened by poor performance may be forced to cut back on parent-related initiatives, partly to increase the amount of funds to be delegated to schools.

Parental involvement and the nurturing of home-school links is an area where local authorities can add value to what schools may otherwise do in isolation, value that parachuted in private service management, for all its contractual effectiveness, may not be able to match. This report contains many examples, from the support that can be offered to bilingual families, to family learning activities, to the burgeoning area of multi-agency support for families. Of course, schools could buy in such services from a private or voluntary contractor, even pooling resources where necessary. Yet a key feature of successful home-school initiatives appears to be use of local knowledge, people and organisations. This report does not intend to predict the future of LEAs. *Yet there must be a central space within their new, probably streamlined role, for the support of home-school initiatives, and general parental involvement in learning.* Such a role would include:

- initiatives to support targeted parent groups (fathers, carers, bilingual families) in targeted schools

- advocacy on behalf of parents (possibly co-ordinating the home-school link workers described below)

- co-ordination of the multi-agency training described below, in tandem with the multi-agency services many local authorities are already putting in place

- support for school-based democratic participation and consultation

It is interesting that many rural LEAs appear to lead the way in home-school support. This may be due to resources, lower deprivation levels and other social factors. Urban authorities can undoubtedly learn from the practices and policies of authorities such as Cambridgeshire, Devon, Suffolk and Warwickshire. Non-urban authorities whose school intakes are including an increasing number of minority ethnic children can also learn from the practices of authorities with experience of multiracial family support.[1]

School level

The most meaningful, sustainable changes in parent-school relationships have to be initiated and implemented at school level. Collaborative relationships need to be fostered that permeate every aspect of a school's culture. Many schools have already taken on this challenging agenda, and are, in Andy Hargreaves' words, 'moving towards the danger of working with parents more openly and effectively... in order to engineer long-term changes in public perception.' (Hargreaves in TES, 12.11.99).

The majority, despite good intentions, still seem to be taking a piecemeal approach to parent-school realtionships. Ofsted's description of secondary schools with a high percentage of ethnic minority pupils appears true for most schools: 'All...see liaison with parents as important. Overall, however, relatively few of the secondary schools have systematic and coherent strategies for improving the quality of relationships between home and school.' (Ofsted, 1999b: 35). Jowett's assertion is also pertinent: 'Schools may have a great many parents providing assistance and see this as a thriving system of parental involvement, whereas very little dialogue or learning by either parents or staff may be taking place.' (Jowett & Baginsky, 1991:201).

Many schools and parents will simply not wish to embrace the agenda of whole-school change. Indeed, a school's relationship with its families may become a new factor in school diversity. At one extreme, there are already schools whose educational roles are embedded with those of parents, from what they teach, to the family and social support offered, to learning opportunities offered to parents. At the other, there could in the future be schools who are deliberately detached from their parents as an integral part of their ethos. Although support for an individual child's learning at home is encouraged, roles and responsibilities are clearly demarcated and relationships kept deliberately distant. Parents could essentially choose their own role in their children's education through their choice of schools. The assumption of this book is that a school at the former end of this axis is more likely to ensure success for all of its pupils than one at the other. But schools and families may prefer to move towards this very different kind of 'danger'.

Changing school structures

> Whatever steps schools take in developing partnerships with families, schools that are most successful are prepared to reconsider all of their established ways of doing business and to restructure in ways that will make them less hierarchical, more personal and more accessible to parents. US Department of Education (Funkhouser & Gonzales, 1997).

Schools who do wish parents to be at the centre of the educational process may need to restructure themselves as institutions. Even with parents' rooms, welcoming signs and 'open door' policies, there is no doubt that schools are organised primarily with staff and students in mind. In particular, large secondary schools can be especially parent-unfriendly. Many secondary schools are already structuring themselves to be more 'primary-like'; either through breaking themselves up into smaller, coherent structures, or through using primary-style teaching methods during Key Stage Three. The Value Added and Achievement project discussed in Chapter 3 shows how systems can be restructured to encourage parental engagement. This book has constantly recognised the inevitability of declining parental involvement through a pupil's school career. What cannot be accepted is that this decline is so rapid, and if occurring at age eleven, premature.

Schools also need to develop policies and practices that are highly flexible and dynamic, to meet the shifting needs of diverse families. As the headteacher of one beacon school said, 'Any given strategy which has been successful with one group of parents in one year, may be quite ineffective in another. We are constantly reviewing our practice and relationships to ensure the most effective ways forward.' The increasing mobility of households, which means that the nature of intakes can vary dramatically from year to year, makes this flexibility even more important.

Schools must also maintain a balance between the perceived need for increased school security and the desire for a school to be as welcoming as possible. The schools that need to look the most welcoming, in order to attract 'not yet reached' parents, are often the ones that most look like fortresses.

Changing professional attitudes

The major barrier to and driver of whole school change is the attitudes and actions of the professionals working in a school. Table 8.1, adapted from a table by Bastiani, charts how professional attitudes may now be and could be framed (Bastiani, 1998: 109).

Table 8.1 Changing professional attitudes: a summary

From	To
Parents are:	*Parents are:*
• a problem/nuisance	• part of the solution
• either not interested or too interested	• with clearly defined rights and expectations on and from them
• take up time that should be devoted to children	• schools cannot reach potential without parental involvement
• teachers and parents should get on with their separate jobs	• teachers and parents have key roles in a shared enterprise
• working with parents is a luxury add-on	• schools have obligations to work with all parents

Home-school relations are:	Home-school relations are:
• mainly for those who work with young or SEN children • peripheral to the main business of a school • concerned with teachers and parents • mainly concerned with individual family-school relationships	• important for all schools and colleges • at the heart of the educational process • necessarily involve pupils • need to be supported by collective parental representation
Improving home-school work is:	Improving home-school work is:
• simply a matter of developing 'good practice' • more about being seen to act • about 'correcting wrong-doing' in home (pathological) • something you learn on the job. training is unnecessary. • a matter for schools to deal with individually local/voluntary initiatives	• a constant learning process • needful of a 'whole-school approach' • about engaging, where necessary, in therapeutic relationships • a key plank of training, INSET and professional development • a matter for national support and

Headteachers as social entrepreneurs

Arguably the most important, if unmeasurable factor in forging a successful home-school relationship is individual dynamism; the source of this dynamism could be any parent or staff member, but is far more likely to be a headteacher. As with virtually every aspect of a school, home-school relations are made or broken by the attitude and actions, policies and practices of the headteacher. Individual teachers can form positive relationships with the parents of their pupils, but a headteacher is crucial to creating school culture that is conducive to such relationships. Although it may seem contradictory, partnership requires proactive leadership, or high quality distributed leadership.

The importance of working with parents is recognised in the National Standards for Headteachers, which states that:

> Effective headship results in parents who enjoy an effective partnership with the school, which contributes to their children's learning; understand and support the work of the school; are kept fully informed about their child's achievements and progress; know how they can support and assist their child's progress. (TTA, 1998a: 5).

This is broad and possibly vague, with good reason. In all the hundreds of schools whose headteachers are developing successful relationships with parents, often as the central plank to school improvement, it is difficult to find common attributes beyond the obvious ones such as openness and a strong personality. Similarly, headteachers can be liabilities to positive relationships for a multitude of reasons. *A new generation of headteachers, groomed to see themselves as social entrepreneurs, could be a greater boost for home-school relations than any other resource, human or capital.*

Teachers as teachers?

Just like schools, teachers cannot be forced to perform a wider social function. Even if the role of the school grows to become centres for community learning and multi-agency family support, there are strong arguments that the role of the teacher should become more clearly defined, as other professionals assume these roles.

However, *all teachers need to recognise that working with parents to support their children's learning is an integral part of their professional role.* Asking teachers to build relationships with parents is not asking them to be social workers. As many teachers prove, building good relationships with parents is a time and energy investment that enables teachers to focus on their core functions: behaviour issues are dealt with far more swiftly and effectively; learning carried out at home is supportive and reinforcing; support and expertise is offered for different aspects of the curriculum; and above all, mutual respect is fostered between all points of the parent-teacher child triangle.

The time that teachers need to nurture relationships with parents needs to be recognised and prioritised at national level. The recent report commissioned by the DfEE into teacher effectiveness acknowledges some aspects of working with parents, yet does not give the status it deserves (DfEE, 2000b). A strong theme emerging from this project is that teachers' time for pastoral work has been squeezed by other priorities since New Labour came to power.

As well as time, three other barriers can be identified: motivation; perceptions of parents' skills; and perceptions of teachers' own skills in working with parents. Clearly, these barriers can never totally disappear, and are subject to many factors. The time barrier is omnipresent, but could be alleviated through use of new technology and a reduction in bureaucratic burdens. The most important policy lever to change attitudes and break down barriers is the training of teachers.

Teacher training

Home-school links are, in theory, already built into all teachers' initial teacher training. The National Standards for Qualified Teacher Status require that teachers must:

- 'have a knowledge of effective ways of working with parents and other carers' (TTA, 1998b: 5)

- 'manage, with support from an experienced specialist teacher if necessary, the work of parents and other adults in the classroom to enhance learning opportunities for pupils.' (TTA, 1998b: 5)

- 'understand the need to liase effectively with parents and other carers' (TTA, 1998b: 12)

In practice, however, this appears a much-neglected feature of ITT. Although there are exceptions, anecdotal evidence reveals that many B.Eds and PGCEs give one lecture throughout a course on the subject. During teaching practices, many schools deliberately cosset students from interactions with parents. As a difficult standard to measure, it may also be ignored by assessors. There is a highly misplaced assumption that the communication skills a teacher learns in relation to pupils will work as effectively with parents.

Teachers are working with parents in spite of their training – not because of it. As with so many strategies, the government may be basing their expectations on the exceptional. Training needs to be improved for the average young teacher, entering his or her first job with only limited experience of communicating with adults on a professional basis. Training for teachers, or lack of it, in home-school issues, was probably the most important message generated from the ATL/IPPR survey, which tapped a wellspring of optimism and enthusiasm for 'training for partnership'. This should encourage action from the GTC and a revitalised TTA that will hopefully be expressed in the forthcoming revised ITT standards. The proposed addition to the standards from the Parenting Education and Support Forum should be considered; this is that 'Teachers should be aware of the vital role of parents and other family carers and of family learning in their children's development and achievement.' *However, knowledge is only part of the issue. In addition, training to develop home-school links should be central to all teacher training.*

It may be that such training will be far more relevant to teachers during their early professional development (between induction and the threshold) when they have a context to apply strategies to, and training can be grounded in real experiences. Brent LEA, for example, organises joint training for teachers, parents and governors. Yet at the moment much of teachers' attitudes to parents are passed on from one generation of teachers to the next, and are often outdated, For instance, the opinion expressed in Crozier's study that 'the uninterested child had uninterested parents' (Crozier, 1997: 193). The ideal timing for such training is probably during the induction year. As training opens up to a greater variety of pathways and providers, this is a real opportunity to place working with parents at the heart of any teacher training and continuing professional development.

There should also be opportunities for teachers to move beyond the minimum standard. *Teachers should be able to specialise in parental involvement, either as an alternative to a subject specialism at primary level, or as an additional specialism at secondary level.*

Multi-agency training
Although teacher training can be improved, there is doubt as to whether such training can ever give future teachers sufficient understanding of the diverse needs and

circumstances of families. Again, even if teachers do not wish to involve themselves in broader family support, it is vital for their learning relationships that teachers gain some understanding and insight into the context of their pupils' home lives (Sinclair & Ghory, 1985: 242).

All professions who work with children and families have similar needs. *There are strong arguments to support a common training requirement for all children's professionals, one module that teachers, learning support assistants, social workers, doctors, nurses, psychologists and youth workers would undertake together.* Such training could forge collective responsibility, and offer cross-profession networking opportunities that feed into the multi-agency services being developed in many areas. The first time in my teaching career that I ever met a social worker, educational psychologist, or Education Welfare Officer was at my first ever child case conference. Aside from such conferences, I never came into professional contact with these other agencies.

Multi-agency training could also encourage a greater flow between these professions. This is clearly a policy proposal that goes far beyond the parent-school field, although it might positively impact on parent-school relationships far more than any isolated training. The idea of multi-agency training will be explored further in IPPR's forthcoming project on the future of the teaching profession.

Other school staff

Whole school thinking about home-school relations must encompass a whole staff group, not only teachers. Learning support assistants, many if not most of whom are parents or grandparents of pupils, often provide key access channels between teachers and parents. On a more formal, specific level, a few schools now employ home-school link workers. Although they may be ex-teachers, their role is unlike that of teachers who are given responsibility for parental involvement. A home-school link worker is employed at the interface between home and school to act as a neutral broker between the two institutions. Such a worker must therefore be deliberately detached from the teaching staff, so that he can act as a trusted intermediary between school, parent and child.

The precise workload of such workers varies between schools; they can focus on support for individual families; liase with community organisations and other local agencies; support families in finding post sixteen pathways to education and employment. If they have one common purpose, it is to act as a conduit to change both school and family's attitudes and behaviour, building bridges with home and school and overcoming barriers and prejudices from both sides.

Currently, home-school link workers are used mainly in schools in disadvantaged areas. In such areas, they provide a crucial access point for parents whose own experience of schooling may have made them negative and unconfident when dealing with their children's schools. Even in these areas, provision for such support is patchy, although most of the EAZs are offering home-school link workers in some form.

> **Box 8.1 The East London Schools Fund: School Home Support Service (UK)**
>
> The East London Schools Fund has been operating since 1982 and Home-School Support Workers are now employed in over 80 schools throughout East London. A national programme is currently being developed through a new charity, School Home Support Service UK. Priorities vary from school to school, but the main purpose is to 'respond quickly to students experiencing difficulties and liaise with their families'. Their work includes:
>
> - Family support
> - Pastoral care
> - Enhancing attendance
> - Prevention of exclusions and truancy
> - Special needs family support
> - Curriculum support
> - Pre-admissions contacts
>
> The link worker also provides a point of contact for other support services, from parenting programmes to welfare issues. Although they work closely with other agencies, one of their identified strengths is that they are independent of other agencies and institutions, including the school itself. They can therefore operate as genuinely 'neutral brokers'.
>
> One of the strengths of the workers is that they are drawn from a variety of backgrounds, from former teachers and social workers to those with fewer qualifications but a wealth of experience. They are often drawn from the community that they serve. Workers are carefully placed to meet the needs of each school. The ELSF also support staff centrally through regular supervision and other training. Staff are funded from several sources, including schools' own budgets.
>
> An evaluation of the service highlighted the following aspects of the ELSF that made the service particularly effective:
>
> - Flexibility of work and breadth of remit
> - Focus on outside-school factors
> - Links with other initiatives (Malek, 1996)
>
> ELSF has recently become involved in providing learning mentors to schools as part of the Excellence In Cities initiative. They are ideally placed to ensure that such a mentoring role attempts to integrate a pupil's family, rather than bypass them.[2]

Funding streams should be made available for schools to employ a home-school link worker. This funding should be available on a twin-track funding system; schools in disadvantaged areas have most need of such additional support, so the resource should be automatically available to them. Eligibility for free school meals is an imperfect proxy, but is still the best available deprivation indicator.

However, home-school link workers should not be confined to the social exclusion arena. Such residualisation would limit their potential national effectiveness. *The long-term aim should be for all schools to have access to such a worker.* A separate fund should be reserved for all other schools to bid for resources to employ home-school link workers. Joint bids from groups of schools, particularly schools with different socio-economic and racial mixes, and secondary and feeder primary school, should be encouraged. Home-school link workers will need support and supervision systems beyond the school, as organisations such as the ELSF provide.

There are three barriers to such a policy. The first is cost. Of all the proposals in this report, this is the one with the largest resource implications. The second is the evidence base. Evaluations of home-school link projects find it difficult to quantify their impact. Their aims are diverse and occasionally imprecise, but this is necessarily so. Although nationally funded, the objectives of home-school workers need to have considerable flexibility. Their aims must extend beyond the short term goals of raising attainment, reducing truancy and exclusions or even increasing participation at progress reviews.

The final barrier is the filling of these thousands of new posts. There is evidence that it is already difficult to fill the newly created vacancies for learning mentors and other school support posts. The skills and commitment required to be a home-school link worker are in short supply. As the East London Schools' Fund has discovered, paper qualifications are often irrelevant compared to other life skills, and existing links with families and the local area. Teachers (previously unattached to the school) should also be given secondment opportunities to take up these posts – the chance to be a home-school link worker could be more enriching than any management MA or NPQH module.

Parents as citizens

One of this report's first observations was that parents' statutory obligations towards their children's schools and learning have remained unchanged. The recommendations made in this report have not challenged this situation, preferring to find voluntary solutions to raise parents' expectations for their children's learning and their role in this. However, a framework for whole school change must also consider how parents must play their part in making this change happen.

It is much more difficult to chart 'changing parental attitudes' as was done above for professionals. There is no 'parental mindset', and certainly not one that can be undone by universal parental training. However, much of that table (particularly the section on 'home-school relations') applies equally to parents. Some additional pointers can be drawn:

Table 8.2 Changing parental attitudes: a summary

From	To
• emphasis on individual, market rights between schools	• emphasis on individual and collective rights in any school
• low trust, high deference	• high trust, low deference
• limited influence through choice	• greater influence through voice
• receiver of ever-more information	• information provider as child-expert
• external exhortation of responsibilities	• self-definition of responsibilities
• consumer (usually passive)	• citizen (as active as time allows)

What is meant by 'parents as citizens'? David Miller has identified three models of citizenship (Pearce & Hallgarten, 2000). In the liberal model, rights and responsibilities are defined but rarely articulated. In the consumer model, citizens' rights, in particular their market rights, are encouraged and expressed on an individual basis. Parental choice is an example of this. The third model is one of collective civic engagement. It is this final model to which this report aspires. A key question remains whether such a model can be reached without the erosion or at least discouragement of parents' individual market rights. This model assumes a new vision of pupils as citizens, one encouraged but not guaranteed by the new citizenship education curriculum.

This report has made few specific recommendations regarding parents who are profoundly disaffected from their children's schooling, or whose only interaction comes in aggressive forms. Part of the reason is that policies should not be built on extremities. For instance, voluntary home school agreements are likely to have little impact on those who are alienated from or hostile to their children's schooling. Yet making them legally binding, as the Conservatives and NAHT recommended, would merely have added to that alienation, while insulting the majority of parents for whom such a contract would be unnecessary (Reported in Advisory Centre for Education Bulletin 87). The family support initiatives described throughout this report should assist some families in reducing disaffection between themselves and their schools. Wider social programmes should also have some effect; the SureStart initiative is probably the most important strategy of all, and needs to be rolled out far more rapidly. However, the most important long term strategy for engaging all parents is working to ensure that all future parents, the pupils in schools now, are motivated by their own experiences of school to engage years later with their own children's schools and learning.

Conclusion

This chapter has attempted to place schools at the heart of new innovations and thinking about parent-school relationships. Its conclusions are as follows:

- The most important way that schools can be supported at the national level to improve relationships with parents is to encourage innovation, through targeted resources and greater 'freedom to modernise' in all areas of school life. One approach would be to develop an 'investors in parents' programme, or build similar criteria into any school's 'investors in people' status.

- There must be a central space within Local Education Authorities' new, probably streamlined role, for the support of home-school initiatives, and general parental involvement in learning.

- Schools who do wish parents to be at the centre of the educational process may need to restructure themselves as institutions.

- Schools also need to develop policies and practices that are highly flexible and dynamic, to meet the shifting needs of diverse families.

- Schools must also maintain a balance between the perceived need for increased school security and the desire for a school to be as welcoming as possible.

- Teachers should be aware of the vital role of parents and other family carers and of family learning in their children's development and achievement. In addition, training to develop home-school links should be central to all teacher training.

- Teachers should be able to specialise in parental involvement, either as an alternative to a subject specialism at primary level, or as an additional specialism at secondary level.

- Options should be explored to develop a common multi-agency training requirement for all children's professionals.

- Funding streams should be made available for schools to employ a home-school link worker. Schools in disadvantaged areas have most need of such additional support, so the resource should be automatically available to them. A separate fund should be reserved for all other schools to bid for resources to employ home-school link workers. Joint bids from groups of schools, particularly schools with different socio-economic and racial mixes, and secondary and feeder primary school, should be encouraged.

Endnotes

1   Suffolk LEA parent partnership scheme has an excellent series of leaflets for teachers on how to work with parents. They were developed based on views collected from parents. Subjects covered include:
    - working with distressed or angry parents
    - telephone talk
    - ways of delivering bad news to parents
    - parents and teachers as co-educators
2   For another example of link workers, see Hallam & Castle, 1999.

Appendices

Appendix 1: Teachers and parents: a survey of teachers' views

Prepared for the Association of Teachers and Lecturers and the Institute for Public Policy Research, March 2000

Executive summary

1.1 Background information

- This report presents the results of a postal survey carried out jointly by the Association of Teachers and Lecturers (ATL) and the Institute for Public Policy Research (IPPR).

- Questionnaires were sent to 2000 ATL members (1000 each to primary and secondary teachers) during January 2000. A 47 per cent response rate was achieved with 936 questionnaires returned. This represents a relatively high level of statistical confidence: plus or minus three percentage points.

- In terms of response there was a near 50/50 split between those teaching in primary and secondary education.

1.7 Home-school relationships and Government education policy

- The majority of respondents agreed (88 per cent either outright or tending to) that unless parental support for learning increases, the Government's aim to raise standards will not be met. Those from secondary education were stronger in their agreement than their primary counterparts.

- Support for the positive role of home-school agreements was also strong, nearly a third (64 per cent) agreed or tended to agree. Again teachers from secondary education were relatively more positive than respondents from primary education.

- Over half (51 per cent) disagreed that SATs help parents understand more about their child's learning. Primary teachers and those between the ages of 21 and 40 responded the most negatively compared to other groups.

- Opinion was divided as to whether current admissions policies are making schools more responsive to parents' wishes with 43 per cent remaining neutral.

- Nearly half (47 per cent) of those responding held no firm opinion on whether New Labour's education policies were helping them work with parents. The remaining responses were overwhelmingly negative (48 per cent disagreeing or tending to). Younger respondents from primary education were the least likely to be negative.

1.8 Parental involvement in children's learning

- Sixty-two per cent of respondents either agreed or tended to agree that the majority of parents want to help their child's learning, but do not know how best to do so. Only 16 per cent expressed any form of disagreement and there was a rough consensus across all types of respondent.

- Respondents differed markedly over whether parent volunteers can make a substantial contribution to raising standards. Around half (52 per cent) expressed their agreement in either of its forms, but nearly a third (29 per cent) remained neutral. Younger teachers and those from primary education were the most likely to view parental volunteers in a positive light.

- Opinion on whether the government should provide parents with leave from work to volunteer was mixed. Again younger respondents and those from primary education were the most likely to support the sentiment.

- Nearly three-quarters (72 per cent) agreed or tended to agree that the legal obligations of parents for their child's education should extend further than at present. Only 16 per cent registered their opposition. Support was most forthcoming from respondents in secondary education and those between the ages of 21 and 40.

1.9 The educational roles of home and school

- Over half (60 per cent) of respondents agreed or tended to agree that the roles and responsibilities of teachers and parents have become too blurred. A higher level of concern was registered from teachers in secondary education than those in primary schooling.

- The concept that parents should have the prime responsibility for PSHE and citizenship was strongly supported. 87 per cent agreed or tended to agree. Nearly nine out of ten (89 per cent) similarly agreed that parents should have prime responsibility for their child's development as an active citizen.

- The groups least likely to support these statements were younger teachers and those from secondary education.

1.10 Home-school communication

- Over half (54 per cent) of respondents agreed or tended to agree that most of their communication with parents was to resolve problem situations. However with nearly a third (31 per cent) expressing disagreement in either form, opinion was relatively divided. Respondents from secondary rather than primary education were more likely to support the statement.

- Similarly there were mixed opinions on whether schools are required to give too much information to parents. Nearly a third (32 per cent) remained neutral with 43 per cent on the disagreement and 26 per cent on the agreement sides.

1.6 Training issues

- There was strong disagreement with the statement that training and professional development had prepared teachers for working with parents. 70 per cent disagreed or tended to disagree and there was near consensus on this across all respondent types.

- Consequently three-quarters of respondents believed that it should form a greater part of initial teacher training and later professional development. The younger age groups were particularly supportive of this idea.

1.7 Parental involvement in school decision making

- Respondents disapproved of all the suggested areas in which parents could become more involved in school decision making. Nearly three-quarters (74 per cent) rejected the assertion that parents should have a greater say in the way that schools are run. Those from the older age groups (40+) were more likely to oppose this than their younger colleagues.

- A lower level of disagreement (55 per cent either tending to or disagreeing outright) was recorded when respondents considered whether increasing the number of parent governors was the best way of increasing parental involvement. Again younger teachers (21-40) were the most likely of the respondent groups to support the statement.

- A similar level of disagreement (56 per cent) was expressed with parents having influence over what is taught in their child's school. Secondary school respondents were relatively more likely to support the notion than those from primary education.

- Seventy-three per cent rejected the assertion that parents should have some say over how school budgets are spent.

- The highest expression of disagreement (77 per cent) was reserved for the statement which suggested that there should be some parental input into the teacher appraisals process. Again older age groups and those from secondary schools were relatively more opposed than their younger and primary based colleagues.

A copy of the full report can be obtained from The CfBT/Lambeth Education Action Zone or can be viewed on IPPR's website www.ippr.org.

Appendix 2: Wednesbury Education Action Zone: Parents as partners

Summary findings of a programme of consultation with Wednesbury parents, May 2000

Introduction

'Parents as Partners' is one of the key ideas underpinning the work of the WEAZ and an important driver for raising achievement and self-esteem among pupils in the area. As part of this drive the WEAZ is keen to ensure that parents' views are brought into the work of the zone from the beginning and used to identify the best ways to develop effective partnerships between schools and parents.

With the Institute of Public Policy Research (IPPR) the WEAZ put together a programme of qualitative and quantitative research designed to understand Wednesbury parents' own views. To establish their perceptions of their levels of involvement in their child's learning at school and in the home and to gauge their responses to new initiatives designed to increase levels of parental involvement.

WEAZ is the first of the Education Action Zones to have actively sought the views and input of parents in its decision-making processes.

Funding for the research with parents was provided by the WEAZ and the Paul Hamlyn Foundation in equal amount.

Summary of research aims

The research aimed to bring together the views of parents from across the 16 schools in Wednesbury:

- to understand their perceptions of their level of involvement in their child's learning
- to explore how easy parents currently find it to get involved with their child's learning – both at school and in the home
- to gauge whether parents would like to further their involvement and, if so, how
- to look at which areas of spending parents prioritise for WEAZ
- to find out what parents think of the different options to develop parental involvement in Wednesbury

Methodology

Parents within WEAZ schools were consulted at two stages:

1. Self-complete questionnaire

A written questionnaire was sent home with every pupil in each of the 16 schools in Wednesbury for parents to complete. Just under 1,500 responses were received.

2. Four focus groups with parents

Two focus groups were held with parents of children at primary schools in Wednesbury and two were held with parents of secondary school children.

Summary of key findings

Parents recognise that developing parent-school partnerships and increasing levels of parental involvement are central factors in raising achievement in Wednesbury.

The response to the questionnaire and enthusiasm of parents attending the focus group discussions suggests that the WEAZ has a good base of parental support to tap into and build on.

Parents' priorities for Wednesbury schools are both material and attitudinal. They are quick to identify gaps in resources and opportunities and place better ICT facilities and more organised activities outside of school high on their priority list. But changing attitudes among all stakeholders – parents, schools and children – is also a major concern and is felt necessary in order to raise expectations, increase commitment and develop a better understanding of each others' needs and limitations.

While a number of parents involved in the research feel involved in their child's learning, genuine 'partnership' between schools and parents in Wednesbury is not currently felt to exist. In moving towards such a partnership model, a major gap identified by parents is a lack of clarity and direction from schools regarding what they expect from parents and how exactly they would like them to be more involved. A need for more directive guidance on what parents should be doing to help their children is highlighted.

Of the options to increase parental involvement, there is most support for:

- pre-school parental development and guidance
- a Parents' Network
- an ICT network linking schools in Wednesbury that is rolled out to parents as well as children

Parents' priorities for the future

Parents' priorities for more material resources:

1. More activities available for children of all ages in Wednesbury – both recreational and educational

    There are very few activities locally for children, there's no park as it was vandalised, no youth centres, there're not enough sports facilities to go round...kids need more things to do outside of school, to get them off the streets.

2. More computer resources

    There is a positive response to the ICT network currently being developed in Wednesbury and a number of parents are also interested in the possiblity of home-loaning computers for parents.

3. More resources and facilities in general

    There needs to be greater access to shared resources – like a resource bank of books, computer programmes and other learning materials.

4. Among parents of primary school children in particular there is a clear desire for an improved teacher: pupil ratio and a feeling that teacher time is currently being stretched.

    Money should be spent on more teachers and smaller classes.

Parents' priorities for attitude change:

1. A change in attitudes among parents, teachers and children

    - Schools need to more openly demonstrate a responsiveness to parents and communicate more clearly what they expect of them.
    - Parents need to develop a better understanding of the demands that schools face and find more ways to support their child's learning outside schools.
    - Children themselves need to work with parents and teachers to generate more enthusiasm and commitment which will in turn raise their own aspirations and ambitions.

    There needs to be a more open relationship between parents and schools – parents should be able to question schools and expect an answer.

2. Better communication between schools and parents

The survey responses highlight a common request from parents for more and better communication with schools. A need for more regular contact with teachers is identified as well as clearer communication of how parents can help.

Parents' current and future involvement in their child's learning

Seventy-seven per cent of those responding to the survey agree with the statement 'I would like to help with my child's learning more than I am doing at the moment'.

However, there are clear barriers to engagement which suggest a need for directive guidelines from schools on how parents can help their children and more flexible ways of working in partnership with parents:

- lack of guidance on how to help
- lack of confidence in supporting homework
- lack of clarity regarding the division of effort and responsibilities
- lack of time

How would parents like to become more involved?

Seventy-three per cent of primary school parents and 64 per cent of secondary school parents responding to the survey say that they would like to be more involved in their child's learning.

The focus groups with parents allowed more time to explore the different options for involvement. Four different models of parental involvement were presented to parents:

1. A Parents Network

The concept of a Parents' Network was well-received by those attending the focus groups – all of whom agreed to be contacted by the WEAZ in the future to develop ways for taking the concept forward. Parents thought it could be used:

- as a means of exchanging ideas and experiences
- to establish links where none exist already
- to take on a lobbying role
- as a central point of contact between schools and parents

2. Supporting learning in the family

Supporting learning in the family receives a positive response, particularly in terms of offering more support to pre-school parents and extending the ENABLE project (a project which provides training and qualifications for parents to support children's reading).

3. Offering more learning and training opportunities for parents themselves

The idea of a community learning and study centre in Wednesbury Library is well received, as is the opportunity to access distance learning materials through home computers. But a number of barriers to parents getting involved in learning and training themselves are identified:

- fitting learning in with work and family commitments
- flexible opening times would be required
- cost
- it requires real motivation

4. Encouraging parents to volunteer in schools

This is the least popular of the options put to parents, although the majority support the principle of the idea. Parents are keen to point out that this model of parental involvement is dependent on parents who don't work or who are able to fit time in around their working life. For the majority of parents it isn't felt to be a realistic option.

Conclusion

There is a strong base of interest and support among parents in Wednesbury that is waiting to be tapped into. The good response to the survey of parents is itself evidence of this and there is a clear indication that parents are willing to get more involved in their child's learning.

The strength of bringing parents together from across the area was highlighted in the focus groups, which provided the means for parents to exchange ideas and experiences across Wednesbury for the first time. It allows parents to identify common goals and begin to develop the motivation to achieve them.

However, it is important to emphasise that the majority of parents involved in the research – those who took the time to complete the survey or attend a focus group discussion – are already 'warm' to the notion of greater parental involvement. These parents must be seen only as a starting point. Equally, if not more important, are those parents currently 'out of the loop', who have little or no contact with schools and who potentially spend little time helping their children learn and develop.

A copy of the full report can be viewed on IPPR's website www.ippr.org.

Appendix 3: Supplementary schooling in the CfBT/Lambeth Education Action Zone

Dr John Bastiani, September 2000

Introduction

This report stems from a small-scale, independent study, commissioned from the Institute For Public Policy Research (IPPR) by the CfBT/Lambeth Education Action Zone, which is based upon a series of discussions and visits that took place during March 2000.

Taking its cue from a brief drawn up by a local Steering Group, the study gives emphasis to two major themes, within an approach that seeks to suggest positive ideas for the development of more effective practice.

- by outlining some of the key features of Supplementary Schools (or Saturday Schools as they are more popularly known, especially amongst parents) within the EAZ, suggesting how they might relate to mainstream schools.

- by identifying ways in which both supplementary schools and mainstream providers, statutory and voluntary, can involve parents, families and the community and strengthen their support for the progress of children for whom they share responsibility.

The study acknowledges some of the tensions, difficulties and problems that characterize the relationships between the different providers and is also sensitive to the needs of hard-pressed families, often living in difficult circumstances. It sets out, however, to reveal a picture – mainly through the words of staff, parents and children themselves – of a largely neglected area of educational life and activity that contains considerable potential to strengthen a community's efforts to educate its children the challenging conditions of inner city life.

It is a cumulative and convincing pattern of overwhelmingly positive benefits and effects that, whilst clear to parents and children themselves, are often unrecognized and unacknowledged by schools and others who are concerned with children's progress and development.

Like other educational evaluations, too, the study begins to throw light upon, and ask questions of, broader issues and processes, such as the conditions within which children, of all ages, learn best and to suggest some of the educative dimensions of family and neighbourhood life.

Selected Quotations

...if partnerships between supplementary schools and mainstream schools make life better for pupils – then that's really worthwhile.
EAZ Project Director

If supplementary schools are the flavour of the month, because of a Labour government, then give them something so they get to the stage where they can develop something effective...or they become an annexe to a school and they will lose their original perspective.
Supplementary School Director

I don't know whether supplementary schools are special. I think they're essential...Schools give the impression that there's only one way to do things, to achieve things. That's nonsense!...

We don't want to replace schools. We just want to work better with them. In partnership.
Director: Supplementary School

Parents said (to me) that kids get a fresh approach, a lot of personal attention and extra help with school work. But there's an extra special ingredient...Two things. The first was having black teachers. And the second was having a shared cultural background and experience. A black perspective and black experience...
Director: Tuition Centre

The kind of thing he (15 year old) was getting from here that he wasn't getting from mainstream school was much more awareness about himself and who he was – in terms of historically and, even more, culturally – where he was coming from.
Parent

The way we see it (here) is if parents are not sufficiently empowered, the impact of what school and other places do with their children, is not maximised... But we know that where this happens, children do much better... And so, empowering a parent is also empowering a child.
Director: Supplementary School

It's because we all have the same interest in the children here. We're working with the children; the system is working for the children. It's the other way

round in mainstream schools...the children are working for the system...They need to work more for the children.
Parent

The school my daughter goes to is predominantly white. I think there's one Asian female and a black female, who works in the kitchen! There's no black man. When children can see people who reflect themselves and these adults are positive role models...it affects their aspirations and their motivations.
Parent

I'd like to see mainstream schools become more child-centred. We pay our taxes; our taxes pay to provide an education for our children and I'd like to see more fighting on behalf of our children's needs and less pandering to central government's targets and numbers games...
Parent

Supplementary schools: a summary of positive features

Saturday Schools are very popular amongst parents and pupils respectively. They are, however, virtually ignored by mainstream schools. They seem to be very effective in catering for a wide range of ages and abilities.

Saturday Schools have a special ethos and identity, which stems from a combination of

- an approach to learning and teaching that is based upon a mix of formal and informal pedagogy and flexible use of time;
- a great deal of individual attention, encouragement and support, from volunteers and mentoring schemes of different kinds;
- strong parental involvement – in the day-to-day running of centres, in their management and in supporting children's work at home;
- more of a family atmosphere than an institutional climate; many parents were formerly pupils themselves; older brothers and sisters continue to help out on a voluntary basis and cooperative rather than competitive values are stressed;
- a grass roots approach that has strong neighbourhood links with individuals and organisations that have relevant knowledge, skill and experience and are willing to share it, on a voluntary basis, for the common good.

Black (and mother-tongue) supplementary schools recognise the importance of shared culture and identity. Black staff provide positive role models of successful learners; they have an experience and understanding of racism in schools and on the streets; they can often draw upon their knowledge of black history and culture in their teaching.

But none of this is news. We have known for many years that children's learning is more likely to thrive in small scale, pupil-friendly communities, characterized by flexible approaches to teaching and learning and underpinned by active family support.

What is new, however, is a recognition of the potential of such experience, largely unrecognised and unacknowledged at present in contributing to, and being supported by, the work of hard-pressed schools in our cities and, especially, in making a positive contribution to the progress and development of black and bilingual pupils, many of whom do not get the education to which they are entitled and which they deserve.

Saturday Schools seem to exhibit a number of the features of partnership, which are a frequent part of educational rhetoric, but less frequently found in practice! Relationships between staff, parents and children seem relatively informal and relaxed (although 'no nonsense!'); staff, volunteers and parents 'get stuck in' to the jobs that need doing, whether it's preparing refreshments, helping kids or fundraising for the centre. Above all the author was forcibly struck by the use of the pronoun 'we' and the adjective 'our' to refer, by parents, to their relationships to their Saturday Schools.

Because of the nature of their sponsoring organisations, two of the three Saturday Schools that were visited have strong community links that reflect their wider interests and activities. This allows them to utilise their longstanding, grassroots knowledge of the local scene, of local needs and circumstances and of local resources, human and material, as a part of their organisation and effort.

Such a summary, which obviously portrays Saturday Schools in a very positive light, also incorporates the twin dangers of overclaiming their virtues, whilst at the same time being overly, or unreasonably, critical of the efforts of mainstream schools working in less than perfect circumstances.

There is also an issue of scale. Supplementary and mother tongue schools, as they currently exist, only work with a small proportion of their school populations! Whilst there is no way of demonstrating whether or not they are typical of their communities as a whole, or of the wider population, one suspects that they are not, (a suspicion voiced earlier by Saturday School parents themselves).

So there are here, as in mainstream schools, issues of opportunity, access and fairness. The active involvement of parents and carers and their consequent empowerment can be seen as both a strategy for tackling educational inequalities and a means of sustaining, or even widening, it. Both can happen.

It is not an issue about whether they are more, or less, effective than mainstream schools or teachers in what they do. Such a claim would be unexaminable, unsustainable and, above all, based on phoney premises – in fact, pointless.

It is, however, to acknowledge the need to discuss how mainstream and supplementary schools and the families of the children for whom they share responsibility, can best work together, in the common interest of children's learning and development.

Some practical proposals for consideration

This small scale study shows some of the advantages and the potential of regarding its supplementary schools as an integral, though distinct, part of the educational provision available to Lambeth children – initially within the EAZ, but subsequently across the Borough.

This immediately raises several issues. Firstly, although the main focus of this report is upon the *educational benefits* of supplementary schools, as seen by a cross section of those involved, it raises a number of important and long standing problems about funding, resources and support, which need to be reconsidered.

Secondly, the provision and development of effective supplementary schools raises issues of availability, access and fairness. How can the positive and beneficial experiences that they provide be made available – in one form or another – to more Lambeth children.

The following proposals are not meant to be comprehensive, but to provide a framework for discussion and planning, that emphasise ways in which mainstream and supplementary schools can work more productively together, tapping into each other's special strengths and experience.

Using this report as a starting point the EAZ should sponsor, monitor and support an additionally funded, time limited (18 months?), joint initiative involving several mainstream and supplementary schools within the Zone.

This would

- identify, implement, monitor, review and evaluate a number of practical initiatives
- model the principles of practical co-operation and joint effort
- emphasise the lessons that can be learned from this experience

As a practical strategy, the initiative could draw upon three different styles of innovation and development.

(i) Action Research

(ii) 'Demonstration Programmes'

(iii)   Pilot Programmes

Some practical objectives

- Sharing and distributing a range of information about each other's work and activities.
- Identifying some possibilities for agreed approaches and complementary activities in teaching and learning; sharing resources and materials.
- Sharing information about the progress and development of individual pupils.
- Tapping each other's skills and experience in relation to topics of special interest and concern, for instance use of drama to explore experience of racism, ethnic music and cultural studies.
- Identifying an agreed approach to the arrangements for recording, assessing and reporting pupil progress.
- Working together to strengthen the co-operation and involvement of black parents in their children's education.
- Making more effective use of INSET, training and development activities in areas of shared concern, for instance literacy development, strengthening anti-racist work.

The EAZ should encourage the LEA to use this study as a catalyst for a wider review of supplementary schools across the Borough. This would need to consider

- issues of funding, management, accommodation and resources
- educational programmes and activities
- links with mainstream schools: joint and dual use

During the last year efforts have been made to identify the job description for the possible appointment of a (part-time) Supplementary Schools Development Worker.

In the light of this study, the merits of such a post are obvious. The report, hopefully, will provide something of a context, a framework and a process for such proposals to be re-examined and for broadly based discussions to be renewed.

The crucial impact of parental involvement in, and support of, children's learning is now both widely recognized and rooted in a growing body of reliable evidence. Working with parents and families is now also a significant element in most areas of the government's social and educational policies and in both the core and additional funding. (For example, Sure Start, Family Literacy, Education Action Zones, SRB Initiatives and the New Deal For Communities).

Given the author's wider experience in this area throughout the UK, home-school links in the EAZ and across the Borough appear to be both understated and underdeveloped. The LEA should initiate and support a cross-borough audit of school-family links in its schools.

At least two further themes have been uncovered in this study

- Giving parents – and supplementary school parents – a greater say in their children's education, at both LEA and school levels
- Identifying ways of sharing practical ideas and experience on the vitally important theme of 'how parents can help their children's learning...'

The first years of the EAZ have inevitably been concerned with setting up a range of provision for the 29 Zone schools, which includes a range of supplementary and complementary activities.

It is now important to look at the interaction of these different activities and attempt to unravel some of the individual and combined effects – both for schools and for pupils with different needs and capabilities.

Accreditation and support

There are already a number of initiatives within the Zone which offer parents, community volunteers and mentors who work in schools, a range of opportunities to get accredited training and support, but it is on an *ad hoc* basis. This could be developed into a co-ordinated approach.

A range of pupil achievement

There is a major contradiction at the heart of the government's educational strategy, which action zones encounter head on. This concerns

- an increasing focus of energy and effort on activities geared to meeting the government's declared and narrow targets of school success, exemplified in National Curriculum test and GCSE scores.
- a corresponding need for additional arrangements and activities, both to compensate for this and to provide opportunities for the broader and fuller growth of attitudes, skills and capabilities, amongst pupils of all ages.

This applies both to pupils in mainstream schools, of all kinds, as a whole and also to particular groups and their differing needs. It is certainly an area in which pupils could benefit enormously from wider discussions involving all those who have a contribution to make to children's learning and development – particularly parents, staff, governors, employers, community groups and, of course, pupils themselves.

Such discussions would have, at their heart, the task of making explicit the range of knowledge, attitudes and skills that pupils should be developing in order to grow up as rounded human beings and effective citizens in the new millennium.

They would also identify practical forms through which these can be recognised and shared in the everyday life and work of both mainstream and supplementary schools and through the ways the various achievements of children and young people are recorded, reported and assessed.

In spite of the many and continuing difficulties that supplementary schools experience at the margins of the educational service, they remain confident about their role, upbeat about their achievements and distinctly optimistic about their futures.

In this, the non-compulsory nature of the enterprise, the mixture of paid and voluntary effort and the underlying commitment to what they are doing, contributes to, and benefits from, the enthusiasm of all those involved. They represent an untapped educational alternative which has wider application and much to teach us.

A copy of the full report can be obtained from The CfBT/Lambeth Education Action Zone or can be viewed on IPPR's website www.ippr.org.

Dr John Bastiani can be contacted on 0115 9143135.

Bibliography

Advisory Centre for Education (1999) *The Communicating School* London: ACE

Advisory Centre for Education Bulletin 87

AFASIC (the Association For All Speech-Impaired Children) research, in *The Independent* (16.5.96)

Alexander T (2000, forthcoming) *Citizenship Schools: Creating the curriculum for a democratic learning society* London: Campaign for Learning

Alexander T (1997) *Family Learning: the foundation of effective learning* London: Demos

Alexander T, Bastiani J and Beresford E (1995) *Home-school policies: A Practical Guide* Nottingham: JET Publications

Apple MW and Zenk C 'American realities: poverty, economy and education' in Apple MW (ed) (1996) *Cultural Politics and Education* Buckingham: Open University Press

ATD Fourth World (2000) *Education: Opportunities Lost* London: ATD Fourth World

Audit Commission (1996) *Trading Places: A Management Handbook on the Supply and Allocation of School Places* Northampton: Belmont Press

Audit Commission & OFSTED (1995) *Lessons in Teamwork: How Governing Bodies can become More Effective* London: HMSO

Ball M (1998) *School Inclusion: The school, the family and the community* London: Joseph Rowntree Foundation

Ball SJ, Bowe R and Gewirtz S (1996) 'School choice, social class and distinction: the realization of social advantage in education' *Journal of Educational Policy*, Vol 11, no 1

Barber M (2000) 'High Expectations for All, No Matter What: Creating a World Class Education Service in England'; speech given to the Smith Richardson Foundation in Washington, in *TES* (7.7.00)

Barber M (1994) *Parents and Their Attitudes to Secondary Schools; interim report* Keele: Keele University Centre for Successful Schools

Basic Skills Agency (1998) *What Works in Secondary Schools: Catching up with Basic Skills* London: Basic Skills Agency

Bastiani J (1989) *Working with Parents: A Whole School Approach* London: NFER-Nelson

Bastiani J and Wolfendale S (2000) *The Contribution of Parents to School Effectiveness* London: David Fulton

Bastiani J and Wolfendale S (eds) (1996) *Home School Work in Britain* London: David Fulton

BBC (2000) 'Parents wary of helping children learn' http://news6.thdo.bbc.co.uk/hi/english/education/features/newsid_184000/184046.stm

Bentley T (1998) *Learning beyond the classroom: education for a changing world* London: Routledge

Better Regulation Task Force (2000) *Red Tape Affecting Headteachers* London: Cabinet Office

Blair M and Bourne J (1998) *Making the Difference: Teaching and Learning Strategies in Successful Multi Ethnic Schools* DfEE Research Brief 59 London: DfEE.

Blair A and Waddington M (1997) 'The home school "contract": regulating the role of parents' *Education and the Law* Vol 9 no 4 Dec 97 pp 291-305.

Blau DM (1999) 'The Effect of Income on Child Development' *Review of Economics and Statistics,* Vol 81, no 2

Bloom B (1964) *Stability and Change in Human Characteristics* New York: John Wiley

Blunkett D (1998) *Partnerships with parents show the way forward.* Department for Education and Employment press release

Boulton P and Coldron J (1996) 'Does the rhetoric work? Parental responses to new right policy assumptions' *British Journal of Educational Studies* Vol 44 no 3

Boulton P and Coldron J (1996 b) 'What do Parents Mean when they Talk About "Discipline" in Relation to their Children's Schools?' *British Journal of Sociology of Education,* Vol 17 no 1

Brannen J, Moss P, Owen C, and Wale C (1996) *Mothers, Fathers and Employment: Parents and the Labour Market in Britain 1984-1994* DfEE Research Report No 10

Brighouse H (2000) *Educational Equality and the New Selective Schooling* London: PESGB

Brighouse H in *The Independent (8/6/2000)*

Brighouse T and Tomlinson S (1991) *Successful Schools: Education and Training Paper No.4* London: Institute for Public Policy Research

Brown P (1990) 'The "Third Wave": education and the ideology of parentocracy' *British Journal of Sociology of Education,* Vol 11 no 1

Burgess A (1998) *Fatherhood Reclaimed* London: Vermilion

Burgess A (1997) *Carlton Parenting Campaign: Fathers* Carlton Television

Cabinet Office (1999) *Modernising Government* London: HMSO

Cabinet Office: Service First Unit (October 1998) *People's Panel: 1st Wave Research* London: Cabinet Office

Cambridgeshire County Council (1999) *Partners in Learning: Building on Experience* Cambridge: Cambridgeshire County Council

Campaign for Learning/NIACE/Scottish Council Foundation (2000) *A Manifesto for Family Learning* London: Campaign for Learning

CEDC (1998) *Successful Schools: Parental Involvement in Secondary Schools: A Good Practice Guide* Coventry: CEDC

Clark A and Power S (1998) *Could Do Better: School Reports and Parents' Evenings: A Study of Secondary School Practice* London: The Research and Information on State Education Trust

Cookson P (1994) *School Choice* London: Yale University

Cowan R and Hallam S (1999) *What do we know about homework*? Institute of Education, University of London

Creese M *et al* (1999) 'Ofsted on Governance: a view from the bridge?' *School Leadership & Management*, Vol 19 no 2

Crouch C (1999) 'Citizenship and markets in recent British education policy' in Crouch C, Eder K and Tambini D (eds) *Citizens Markets and States* Oxford University Press 2000

Crozier G (1998) 'Is it a Case of "we know when we're not wanted?": The Parents' Perspective on Parent Teacher Roles and Relationships'. Paper from the *British Educational Research Association Annual Conference*, Belfast 1998 p1

Crozier G (1997) 'Empowering the Powerful: a discussion of the interrelation of government policies and consumerism with social class factors and the impact of this upon parent interventions in their children's schooling' *British Journal of Sociology of Education* Vol 18 no 2

Crozier G (1996) 'Black Parents and School Relationships: A Case Study' *Educational Review, 48 (3)*

The Daily Mail (2.10.99) 'The School that shames this Country's Education System'

David M (1995) 'Parental wishes versus parental choice' *History of Education* Vol 24 no 3

David ME *et al* (1994) *Mother's Intuition? Choosing Secondary Schools*. London: Falmer Press

Deem R, Brehony K, and Heath S (1995) *Active Citizenship and the Governing of Schools* Buckinghamshire: Open UP

DeRijke J (2000) *Investors in Parents: Interim Report* PTA Devon

DES (1991, updated 1994) *The Parent's Charter* London: DES

DETR (1998) *Focus on personal travel* London: DETR

DETR (1998) *Modern Local Government: in touch with the people* (Local government White Paper) London: The Stationary Office

DfEE (2000a) *Statistical First Release: Admission Appeals for Maintained Primary and Secondary Schools in England 1998 – 1999*

DfEE (2000b) *A Model of Teacher Effectiveness* A Report by Hay McBer to the Department for Education and Employment – June 2000

DfEE Circular 10/99 *School Inclusion: Pupil Support* London: DfEE

DfEE (1999a) 'The Training and Development of Flexible Workers' *Research Brief: Report No. 118* August 1999 London: DfEE

DFEE (1999b) *Learning Elements of the Single Regeneration Budget* London: DfEE

DfEE (1999c) *Meet the Challenge: Education Action Zones* London: DfEE

DfEE (1999d) *Statistics of Education: Survey of Information and Communications Technology in Schools 1999* London: The Stationary Office

DfEE Press Release (4.8.99) *Events and Historical Figures Central to History Curriculum – Morris* London: DfEE

DfEE press release (31.8.99) *Home-School Agreements Strengthen School Partnerships with Parents* London, DfEE

DfEE (1998a) *Home-School Agreements: Guidance for Schools* London: DfEE

DfEE (1998b) *Circular no 2/98: Reducing the Bureaucratic Burden on Teachers* London; DfEE

DfEE (1998c) *Homework: Guidelines for Primary and Secondary Schools* London:DfEE

DfEE (1998d) *Teachers: meeting the challenge of change* (technical consultation document) London: DfEE

DfEE (1998e) *Education Development Plans* London: DfEE

DfEE Circular 12/98 *Schools Admissions: Interim guidance* London: DfEE

DfEE (1997a) *Connecting the Learning Society* London: TSO

DfEE (1997b) *Excellence in Schools* London: TSO

DfEE and MORI (1999) *Parents and Schools* London: DfEE (Unpublished report)

Dosanjh JS and Ghuman PAS (1997) 'Asian Parents and English Education – 20 years on: a study of two generations' *Educational Studies* Vol 23 no 3 p459

Echols F H and Williams J D (1992) *Scottish Parents and Reasons for School Choice* Vancouver: University of Columbia

Edexcel (2000) *Standards: Parents Views* London: Edexcel

Edwards R, Alldred P and David M (2000) 'Children's Understanding of Parental Involvement in education' *ESRC Children 5-16 Research Briefing* 11

Einzig H and Wolfendale S (eds) (1999) *Parenting Education and Support: New opportunities* London: David Fulton.

Elkinsmyth C and Bynner J (1994) *The basic skills of young adults: some findings from the 1970 British Cohort Study*, a report prepared by Social Statistics Research Unit for the Adult Literacy and Basic Skills Unit (ALBSU): London

Epstein J (1992) *School and Family Partnerships (Report No.6)* Baltimore: Johns Hopkins University, Center on Families, Communities, Schools and Children's Learning

Ermisch J and Francesconi M (1998) *Mother's Employment, Lone Motherhood and Children's Achievements as Young Adults* Working Paper 98 (9) ESRC Research Centre on Micro-Social Change

Ermisch J and Francesconi M (1997) *Educational Choice, Families and Young People's Earnings* Working Paper 97 (6) ESRC Research Centre on Micro-Social Change

Eurydice (1997) *The Role of Parents in the Education Systems of the European Union* Brussels: European Unit of Eurydice

The Evening Standard, 29/9/1999: 'The do-it-yourself school of learning'

Family Action Centre (1997) *The FatherCare Initiative: Getting Dads Involved in Schools* University of Newcastle.

Family Policy Studies Centre (2000) *Family Change: Guide to the issues* Family Briefing Paper 12 London: FPSC

Fantini M (1980) 'Community participation; alternative patterns and their consequence on educational achievement' *American Educational Research Association Meeting*

Feinstein L (1998) 'Which Children Succeed and Why: What are the keys to success for British school children?' *New Economy* June 1998 Vol 5 no 2

Feinstein L and Symons J (1999) 'Attainment at Secondary School' *Oxford Economic Papers*, Vol 51, no 2

Funkhouser, J. Gonzales, M. (1997) *Family Involvement in Children's Education: Successful local approaches* Washington: US Department of Education Office of Educational Research and Improvement

Gewirtz S, Ball S J and Bowe R (1995) *Markets, choice and equity in education* Buckingham: Open UP

Giddens A (1991) *Modernity and self-identity: self and society in the late modern age* Cambridge: Polity Press

Gillborn D (1998) 'Racism, selection, poverty and parents: New Labour, old Problems?' *Journal of Education Policy*, Vol 13, no 6

Glenn CL (1995) *Educational Freedom in Eastern Europe* Washington DC: Cato Institute

Gopnick A, Meltzoff A, and Kuhl P (2000) *How Babies Think* Berkeley, CA: Weidenfeld & Nicolson

Gorard S and Fitz J (2000) 'Investigating the determinants of segregation between schools', *Research Papers in Education*, Vol 15 no 2

Gorard S (1999) 'Well. That about wraps it up for school choice research: a state of the art review' *School Leadership & Management*, Vol 19 no 1

Graham J and Bowling B (1995) *Young People and Crime: self-reported offending among 14-25 year olds in England and Wales* Home Office Research Study 145, London: Home Office

Granovetter M (1973) 'The strength of weak ties', *American Journal of Sociology of Education*, 78

Gray J (2000) *Causing Concern but Improving: A Review of Schools' Experiences* DfEE Research Brief 188

Gregg P and Machin D (1998) *Child Development and Success or Failure in the Youth Labour Market* London: LSE Centre for Economic Performance

Hallam S and Castle F (1999) *Evaluation of a School-Home Liaison Project – London Diocesan Board for Schools* London: Institute of Education

Halpin D (1999) Speech to NUT Conference on Education Action Zones

Halpin D (1998) *Democracy, inclusive schooling and the politics of education* Paper presented to the British Educational Research Association, August 1998

Hannon P (1993) 'Conditions of learning at home and in school' in *Ruling the Margins* London: London University Institute of Education

Hannon P (1995) *Literacy, Home and School: Research and Practice in Teaching Literacy with Parents* London: Falmer Press

Hardyment C (1983) *Dream Babies: Child Care from Locke to Spock* London: Cape

Hargreaves A (1999) 'A Social Movement for Public Education?' in *The Times Educational Supplement* (12.11.99)

Hargreaves D (1997) 'A Road to the Learning Society' in *School Leadership and Management* Vol 17 no 1 1997

Harkness S 'Working 9 to 5' in Gregg P and Wadsworth J (eds) (1999) *The State of Working Britain* Manchester: Manchester University Press

Harris JR (1998) *The Nurture Assumption* New York: The Free Press

Haskey J (1998) 'Families: their historical context, and recent trends in the factors influencing their formation and dissolution' in David m (ed) *The Fragmenting Family: Does it Matter?* London: Institute of Economic Affairs

Heyneman SP (1997) 'Educational Choice in Eastern Europe and the Former Soviet Union: A Review Essay' *Education Economics*, Vol 5, no 3

Hinds T, Martin J, Ranson S and Rutherford D (1992) *The Annual Parents' Meeting: Towards a Shared Understanding* University of Birmingham: A Report to the DFE

HM Treasury (1999) *The Modernisation of Britain's Tax and Benefit System: Tackling Poverty and Extending Opportunity* London: HM Treasury

Hobcraft J (1998) *Intergenerational and Life Course Transmission of Social Exclusion* London: Centre for Analysis of Social Exclusion

Holden C, Hughes M, and Desforges C (1994) 'Parents and Entitlement: a fair deal for all?' *Educational Review*, Vol 46, no 2

Home Offfice (1999) *Freedom of Information Bill* London: The Stationary Office

The Home Office (1998) *Supporting Families: A Consultation Document* London: HMSO

House of Commons Education and Employment Select Committee (1999) *Fifth Report: The Role of School Governors* London: TSO

Howarth C, Kenway P, Palmer G and Miorelli R *Monitoring Poverty and Social Exclusion 1999* York: Joseph Rowntree Foundation/New Policy Institute

Islington Council Policy Committee (2000) *A Fresh Start for Islington Education*

Jencks C and Mayer SE (1990) 'The Social Consequences of Growing Up in a Poor Neighbourhood' in Lawrence J, Lynn E, and McGeary M G H *Inner-City Poverty in the United States* Washington DC: National Academy Press p137

Jowett S and Baginsky M (1991) 'Parents and Education – issues, options and strategies' *Educational Research*, Vol 33, no 3

Katz Y (1997) 'Effective Collaboration between teachers and parents in Israel' *Pastoral Care*, Dec 1997

Keys W and Fernandes C (1990) *A Survey of School Governing Bodies: a report for the DES* London: DES

Labour Force Survey, Spring 1998

Lake M (1995) 'Who are the children who fail?' *Managing Schools Today* 9/95

Lansdown G (1995) *Taking Part. Children's Participation in Decision Making* London: IPPR

Leadbeater, C in *The Times Education Supplement* (25.6.99) p15

Lloyd E (ed) (1999) *Parenting matters: what works in parenting education?* Ilford, Essex: Barnardo's

MacBeath J (1999) *Schools Must Speak for Themselves: The Case for School Self Evaluation* London: Routledge

MacBeath J and Weir D (1991) *A Digest of UK Surveys and Polls on Parents' Teachers' and Pupils' Attitudes to School 1985 – 90* Jordanhill College of Education

MacBeth A (1989) *Involving Parents: effective parent-teacher relations* Oxford: Heinemann Educational

Malek M (1996) *Making Home-School Work. Home-school work and the East London Schools Fund* London: National Children's Bureau

Mayer S (1997) *What Money Can't Buy: Family Income and Children's Life Chances* Cambridge, MA: Harvard University Press

McCarraher L (1998) *Family Viewing: A report of the research project into parents, children and the media* London: Parenting Education & Support Forum

McCormick J (1999) *Family Learning: Parents as Co-Educators* London/Glasgow: IPPR/SCF

McKenna M and Williams J D (1998) 'Co-operation between Families and Schools: What Works in Canada' *Research Papers in Education*, Vol 13, no 1

McLanahan S S (1997) 'Parent Absence or Poverty: Which Matters More?' in Duncan G J and Brooks-Gunn J (eds) *Consequences of Growing up Poor* New York: Russel Sage Foundation.

McMillan R (1999) *Parental Pressure and Competition: An Empirical Analysis of the determinants of Public School Quality* Stanford, USA: Stanford University

Marsiglio W (1991) 'Parental engagement activities with minor children' *Journal of Marriage & Family*, Vol 53, no 4

Mental Health Foundation study (1999), in *The Guardian* 24/6/99

Merttens R and Vass J (eds) (1993) *Partnership in maths: parents and schools, the IMPACT project* London: Falmer

Milgram RM and Hong E (1996) 'Preferred and actual homework style: a cross-cultural examination' *Educational Research*, Vol 41, no 3 Winter 99 pp 251-265

Milliband D (1991) *Markets, Politics and Education: Beyond the Education Reform Act* London: The Institute for Public Policy Research

Moore K *et al* (1999) *A Birth Cohort Study: Conceptional and Design Considerations and Rationale* Washington: National Centre for Education Statistics

Mortimore P (1988) *School Matters: The Junior Years* London: Open Books

Mortimore P, Thomas S, Sammons P, Owen C and Pennell H (1994) *Assessing school effectiveness: developing measures to put school performance in context* London: Institute of Education, International School Effectiveness & Improvement Centre

Mortimore P and Whitty G (1997) *Can school improvement overcome the effects of disadvantage?* London: Institute of Education

Moser C (1999) *A Fresh Start: Improving Literacy and Numeracy* London: DfEE

Mountfield A and Eastwood N (2000) *School Fundraising in England: A Directory of Social Change Research Report* London: Directory of Social Change

Muller C (1993) 'Parent Involvement and Academic Achievement: An Analysis of Family Resources Available to the Child' in Schnieder B and Coleman J S *Parents, Their Children, and Schools* Boulder: Westview Press

Munn P (ed) (1993) *Parents and Schools: Customers, Managers or Partners?* London: Routledge

Munn P (1998) *Parental influence on School Policy: Some evidence from research* Moray House Institute of Education, Heriot-Watt University

NAHT survey in *The Guardian* (7.4.00)

National Association of Governors and Managers survey in The Times Educational Supplement (11.6.99) p6

National Commission on Education *(1994) Learning to succeed* London: Heinemann

National Consumer Council/Service First (1997) *Involving Users: Improving the Delivery of Education* London: Service First Unit

National Support Project for Secondary Schools (2000) *how to.... Provide training for volunteers and learning support assistants* London: Basic Skills Agency

Nechyba T, McEwan P and Older-Aguilar D (1999) *The Impact of Family and Community Resources on Student Outcomes: An assessment of the international literature with implications for New Zealand* Stanford, USA: Stanford University

NFER study of Basic Skills Agency Family Literacy Demonstration (1997) London: Basic Skills Agency

Nias J (1981) 'Highstones: Mirror Images and Reflections: A case study of the developing relations of a new school' in Bridges D, and Nias J *Case Studies in School Accountability Volume II* Cambridge: Cambridge Institute of Education in association with Homerton College

O'Connor M (1994) *Giving Parents a Voice* London: The Research and Information on State Education Trust

OECD (1997) *Parents as Partners in Schooling* London: OECD

OECD (1994) *School: a Matter of Choice* Paris: OECD

Ofsted (2000) *Framework 2000: Inspecting Schools:* London: OFSTED

Ofsted (1999) *Raising the Attainment of Minority Ethnic Pupils* London: OFSTED

Ofsted (1997) *From Failure to Success – How Special Measures Are Helping Schools Improve* London: OFSTED

Ofsted (1995a) *Framework for Inspection* London: HMSO

Ofsted (1995b) *Reporting Pupils' Achievements* London: HMSO

Ouston J & Hood S (2000) *Home-School Agreements: A true partnership?* London: The Research and Information on State Education Trust

Pearce N and Hallgarten J (eds) (2000) *Tomorrow's Citizens: Critical Debates in Citizenship and Education* London: IPPR

Plomin R and Petrill S (1997) 'Intelligence: What's New?' *Intelligence,* Vol 24, p31

Pugh G, De'Ath E and Smith C (1994) *Confident parents, confident children: policy and practice in parent education and support* London: National Children's Bureau.

Reay D (1996) 'Contextualising Choice: social power and parental involvement' *British Educational Research Journal,* Vol 22, no 5

Reich R (1998) 'Light blue touch paper' in *The Observer* (15.3.98)

Reid M I (1984) 'School reports to parents: a study of policy and practice in the secondary school' *Educational Research,* Vol 26, no 2

Research and Information on State Education Trust (1997) *Complaints in Schools: A Report and Model General Complaints Procedure* London: RISE

Rice P (1996) *Further Education or the Job Queue* Mimeo: University of Southampton

Robertson D and Symons J (1996) *Do Peer Groups Matter? Peer Group Versus Schooling Effects on Academic Attainment* London: LSE Centre for Economic Performance

Robson E and Dyson A (1999) *School, Family, Community: Mapping school inclusion in the UK* Leicester: Youth Work Press and The Joseph Rowntree Foundation

RSA/NAHT (1992) *A Willing Partnership: Project Study of the Home-School Contract or Partnership* London: RSA

RSL/TES survey in *The Times Educational Supplement (*10.1.97)

Runnymede Trust (1998) *Improving Practice: A whole school approach to raising the achievement of African Caribbean youth* The Runnymede Trust in association with Nottingham Trent University

Rutter M and Madge N (1976) Cycles of Disadvantage London: Heinemann

Sammons P, Hillman J, and Mortimore P (1995) *Key Characteristics of Effective Schools: A Review of School Effectiveness Research.* London: Ofsted & Institute of Education

Schweinhart LJ and Barnes DP (1993) *The High/Scope Perry Pre-school Curriculum Models through age 27* High/Scope Educational Foundation, Ypsilanti: Michigan

Scottish Consumer Council (2000) *Parents as partners in Scottish Education: Developing parent representation through a national parents' body. A discussion paper* Glasgow: Scottish Consumer Council

Scottish Council Foundation (2000, forthcoming) *Beyond Disappointment: Public Involvement and Better Communities* Edinburgh: SCF

Sinclair RL and Ghory WJ (1985) 'Curriculum Connections' in Fantini M and Sinclair R (eds) *Education in School and Non-School Settings* Chicago: University of Chicago Press

Sly F (1994) 'Mothers in the labour market' *Employment Gazette* November.

Smedley D (1995) 'Marketing secondary schools to parents – some lessons from the research on parental choice' *Education Management and Administration,* Vol 23, no 2

Social Exclusion Unit Policy Action Team 11 (2000) *Schools Plus: Building Learning Communities* London:DfEE

Stoer SR and Cortesao L (1999) 'The Reconstruction of Home/School Relations: Portuguese conceptions of the "responsible parent"' *International Studies in Sociology of Education,* Vol 9, no 1

Straw J (1991) *Labour's Charter for Parents* London: The Labour Party

Sui-Chu EH and Williams JD (1996) 'Effects of Parental Involvement on Eighth-Grade Achievement' *Sociology of Education,* Vol 69 pp126-141

Tabberer R (1995) *Parents' Perceptions of OFSTED's Work* Slough: NFER

Teacher line survey *The Times Educational Supplement* (19.5.00)

Tizard B and Hughes M (1984) *Young children learning: talking and thinking at home and at school* London: Fontana

Tomlinson S (1991) 'Home-School Partnerships' in *Teachers and Parents:* London: IPPR

TTA (1998a) *National Standards for Headteachers* London: TTA

TTA (1998b) *Standards for Initial Teacher Training* London: Teacher Training Agency

Tulloch M (1990) *School choice and appeals* London: Advisory Centre for Education.

UNICEF (1993) *Child Neglect in Rich Nations* New York: UNICEF

Vincent C (1996) 'Parent Empowerment? Collective action and inaction in education' in *Oxford Review of Education,* Vol 22, no 4

Vincent C, Martin J and Ranson S (2000) *Little Polities: Schooling Governance and parental participation.* Final report to the ESRC.

Walker B M (1998) 'Meetings without Communication: a study of parents' evenings in secondary schools' *British Educational Research Journal,* Vol 24, no 2

Warwickshire County Council (1999) 'Working with Parents' *Name and Acclaim: Successful Strategies for School Improvement* Issue 3 Autumn 1999

Waslander S and Thrupp M (1997) 'Choice, competition and segregation' in Halsey AH et al (eds) *Education, Culture, Economy and Society* Oxford: OUP

Weinberger J (1996) *Literacy goes to school: the parents' role in young children's literacy learning* London: Paul Chapman

West A, David M, Noden P, Edge A and Davies J (1996) *Choices and Expectations at Primary and Secondary Stages in the State and Private Sectors* conference paper prepared for BERA: Lancaster

Weston P and Ofsted (1999) *Homework: Learning from practice* London: The Stationary Office

Whitty G, Halpin D and Power S (1998) *Devolution and Choice in Education: the school, the state and the market* Buckingham: Open UP

Wilkinson H (ed) (2000) *Family Business* London: Demos

Wolfendale S (1992) *Empowering parents and Teachers* London: Cassell

Wolfendale S (1995) 'A Review of Approaches facilitating home-school partnership in recording progress' *TOPIC* issue 14

Wolfendale S (1997) *Working with parents of SEN children after the Code of Practice* London: David Fulton

Worpole K *et al* (2000, forthcoming) *Linking Home and School* London: Comedia

Wragg EC, Wragg CM, Haynes GS and Chamberlin RP (1998) *Improving Literacy in the Primary School* London: Routledge

Wylie C and Thomson J (1999) *Competent Children at 8: Families, Early Education, and Schools* Wellington, New Zealand: New Zealand Council for Educational Research

Zeldin T (1995) *An Intimate History of Humanity* London: Minerva